*To my wife Cecile
and my children Kristie, Bill, John, Tom, and Michael
with love*

Billy Tauzin

THE
NATIONAL RETAIL SALES TAX

Why America Should Abolish the Federal Income Tax Code and the IRS, and Adopt a NATIONAL RETAIL SALES TAX

CONGRESSMAN
BILLY TAUZIN

ISBN Number 1-57980-308-3

Published and for sale by
CLAITOR'S PUBLISHING DIVISION
3165 S. Acadian at I-10, P.O. Box 261333
Baton Rouge, LA 70826-1333
Tel: 800-274-1403 (In LA 504-344-0476)
Fax: 504-344-0480
e mail: CLAITORS@claitors.com
Internet address:
World Wide Web: http://www.claitors.com

Throughout our history, governments, both large and small—autocratic, democratic and totalitarian—have tried to shape destiny...to change peoples' lives. But in the end, we, the people, invariably manage to change government instead.

Today we are seeing that happen time and time again. Americans are becoming increasingly fed up with an out-of-control Internal Revenue Service and a punitive income tax system. As a result, people all across the country are fighting back, demanding fundamental reform.

Since writing this book, our efforts to change Washington have gained momentum. Just consider:

- During the past nine months, millions of Americans have attended, read news accounts, or watched on television the historic Armey-Tauzin "Scrap the Code" debates held in more than 30 cities across the nation.

- On June 17, 1998, the U.S. House of Representatives voted to sunset the present income tax code effective December 31, 2001, forcing Congress to come up with a simpler, fairer system for all Americans.

- On June 12, 1998, the Texas Republican Party, at its annual convention, adopted a platform, position, calling for the abolishment of both the IRS and the income tax. They would be replaced with a national retail sales tax, which I will describe in detail in this book.

- On July 2, 1998, nearly 200,000 reform-minded citizens in Arizona banded together to force a November ballot initiative on the future of the income tax. If approved, the referendum (The IRS Elimination Pledge Act of 1998) calls on Congress to scrap the income tax code and adopt a national consumption tax.

- In Jerry Jasinowski's excellent book, *The Rising Tide*, Harvard economist Dale Jorgenson writes that under a national retail sales tax, "producers' prices would fall by almost 25 percent relative to prices under an income tax...exports would jump 29 percent." This further strengthens arguments made in this book that consumers, in the long run, will benefit greatly when America has the courage to abolish both the IRS and the income tax.

Clearly, the momentum for change is beginning to build. As a small boy growing up in Chackbay, Louisiana, I used to take rocks and skip them across the bayou. It was fascinating to watch as ripples spread slowly across the water. Well, today I am throwing rocks again. But this time they are aimed at an oppressive IRS and unfair income tax.

And guess what? I see the same kind of ripples spreading across America today, thanks to people like you!

Acknowledgments

This book is dedicated to the memory of my father, Wilbert "Boone" Tauzin. Dad was one of those rare Americans, who never made a credit purchase, never owned a credit card, and never signed a mortgage. He believed that he only needed something when he could afford to buy it. He built his home with his own hands—wired it, plumbed it, and remodeled it as our family grew. He reared us to know the value of working hard and contributing to our community. He would have enjoyed reading this book and knowing that the only son he raised cherished liberty enough to carry on the fight to rid our country of a freedom-robbing tax code.

I also wish to dedicate this book to the courageous life of my mother, Enola M. Tauzin, who twice survived the vicious scourge of cancer and today lives on as a testament to God's merciful grace on earth.

The effort to repeal the income tax code and abolish the Internal Revenue Service will require the courage and perseverance of Enola and the tireless work ethic of Boone Tauzin. The success of that effort will be the best gift my generation can leave to the next.

Contents

The National Retail Sales Tax

✔ **Eliminates the income tax**

✔ **Closes the IRS**

✔ **Exposes hidden consumer taxes**

✔ **No individual tax returns and no net business compliance costs**

✔ **No income tax withholding; take-home pay goes up**

✔ **Rewards savings and investment**

✔ **No loopholes for the rich**

✔ **Fair treatment for housing and the poor**

✔ **Gives U.S. exports a boost**

FIVE REFORM-MINDED lawmakers, U.S. Representatives Dan Schaefer (R-Colorado), Charlie Norwood (R-Georgia), Mike Crapo (R-Idaho), Ron Packard (R-California), and Billy Tauzin (R-Louisiana) tossed the dreaded IRS code into Boston Harbor on April 15, 1997, in a modern-day act of tax defiance. (Photo by Associated Press)

"The hardest thing in the world to understand is the income tax."

Albert Einstein

CHAPTER 1

An American Tea Party

The history of our country can be said to have started at a number of points. Some would argue that we should look all the way back to the Siberian land bridge. Others would point to Scandinavian visits; still others would credit Columbus or the Jamestown settlers. But, I believe the birth of America dates back to the time when a small band of colonial patriots known as the Sons of Liberty gathered at a tavern in Boston Harbor, called the Green Dragon, and plotted an act of civil disobedience that we now remember as the Boston Tea Party.

This band of disobedient rascals gave birth to liberty in America. Their action at the lowest, least powerful level of political existence created the idea that people who colonized the North American continent were to be determinants of their own futures. They, the taxpayers— not the tax collector—would determine their own fate, a concept as applicable to a distant king and Parliament in Great Britain as to the tax collector government, which they would later create for themselves in the New World.

What a remarkable idea! Taxpayers, historically appearing in the form of vassals, serfs, and subjects, would no longer put up with tax collectors determining their future.

The paltry English tax on tea seems so insignificant today that it's hard to believe it became the focus of so profound an idea. But it did. And if a small tax on tea could light such a brilliant flame within the hearts of our forefathers, what a raging conflagration our monstrous income tax code should ignite today. Has the American tax collector become more determinant of our future than we, the taxpayers, should ever permit? Has the American income tax system, and its collector, the Internal Revenue Service, become so offensive to the successful pursuit of individual freedom and liberty that we now serve a new king, a new master of our fate? Given a real choice today, would taxpayers approve of such a burdensome, oppressive and counterproductive tax system—particularly when there are such better choices available? I, for one—and I believe millions of people like me—can sum up the answer to these questions with a simple declaration:

It Is Time For Another American Tea Party.

I believe it is useful to remember in more detail the events of that first expression of taxpayer self-determination—that first tea party in Boston, Massachusetts.

BOSTON TEA PARTY

Hanging! That was the penalty prescribed by the English Crown for the crime of treason during the American Colonial years. However, hanging was not the end of it. Following the hanging, the treasonous citizen would have "his guts drawn from him like a chicken and be cut into four quarters to be hung in the drying wind and sun."

That was the penalty awaiting any colonist who dared challenge the authority of the English government over something as seemingly inconsequential as a small import tax on tea. No wonder, then, that the men who gathered at the Green Dragon on that rainy day in Boston Harbor, December 15, 1773, carefully arranged for Mohawk Indian war paint and blankets to cover the identities of the actual participants in the historic Boston Tea Party. For many of those early patriots, history will never credit what they did that day. They remain anonymous. But history has recorded the names of most of the principal organizers, who, literally, placed their personal lives and fortunes at great risk to make a single point: Taxation without representation is inherently wrong.

Some of the names are familiar. Paul Revere was there. So was John Hancock, along with lesser notables such as Dr. Joseph Warren, Captain Andrew McIntosh, Dr. Benjamin Church, William Milieux, Joseph Quincy, Benjamin Edes, and Thomas Melville, grandfather of Herman Melville, the author of *Moby Dick*. The man who actually commanded the tea party was Lendell Pitts, but the undisputed leader of the Sons of Liberty that day was Sam Adams.

In a small apartment in the Green Dragon, over punch and tobacco, this group laid out their plans for the next day's rebellious activities.

2

The immediate object of their ire was the British ship Dartmouth carrying 114 chests of English tea, the British brig Beaver and another tea ship Eleanor, all anchored near Griffins Wharf inside Boston Harbor. The larger and more profound reason for their anger was the passage by the British Parliament on May 10, 1773, of the Tea Act, which compounded the effect of a three-penny tax with a monopoly concession to the British East India Company to sell tea in America. It was as much the monopoly as the three-penny tax that inflamed patriot hearts. The tea tax was already six years old and three years of relative calm had elapsed since the infamous Boston Massacre of March, 1770. The East India monopoly was the bigger problem, for it put colonial importers out of business. Sam Adams was quick to point out that if the British Parliament could create tea monopolies, it could do the same for every other import commodity. The near-dead issue of the tea tax was easily resurrected and was a more understandable issue for the average colonist.

Across the colonies, protests and acts of civil disobedience had followed. In New York and Philadelphia, British tea ships were turned back. Boston was different. In Boston, one of the two local firms designated by the East India monopoly to import tea into Boston was none other than that of Thomas and Elijah Hutchinson, sons of Massachusetts Governor William Hutchinson. Governor Hutchinson would not yield to the demands of the Sons of Liberty that the ships be sent back to England. Nothing could have better served Sam Adams' desire for a confrontation.

On March 29 and 30, 1773, Sam Adams and the Sons of Liberty helped assemble more than 5,000 people at a mass meeting held first at Faneuil Hall and then the Old South Meeting House in Boston. The assembly called itself "the Body" and each day unanimously demanded that the three tea ships return to England. The Committees of Correspondence were employed to coordinate and communicate, and the Sons of Liberty operated as shock troops to keep the issue inflamed for the next several weeks.

On that fateful morning of December 16, 1773, at 10 o'clock, the Body—estimated between 5,000 and 7,000 men—assembled in the Old South Meeting House and once again ordered the ships' owner to send his tea back to England and instructed him to travel the seven miles to the Governor's house at Milton to seek permission to sail. At 5:45 p.m., the owner returned to the Body to repeat the Governor's refusal. At that point, Sam Adams spoke the words that signaled the call to action. "This meeting," he said, "can do nothing more to save the country."

From the nearby Edes and Gill Printing Shop came men in Mohawk war paint and blankets, whooping and hollering carrying axes and hatchets. They gathered and fell into orderly columns, those behind them cheered on the protesters.

When they were done, at about 9 p.m., many chests of tea—about 90,000 pounds of this staple of English life—had been dumped into the waters of Boston Harbor. The government of Great Britain responded by virtually annulling the Massachusetts charter, replacing Governor Hutchinson with General Thomas Gage and moving in British troops. Those tea leaves spread upon the waters of Boston Harbor became the seeds of revolution. The Boston Tea Party led directly to Lexington and then to Concord and, eventually, to the Declaration of Independence.

ANOTHER AMERICAN TEA PARTY

On April 15, 1997, four Republican members of Congress (Dan Schaefer of Colorado; Mike Crapo of Idaho; Charles Norwood of Georgia; and Ron Packard of California) accompanied me to Boston Harbor, and there we dumped a tea chest filled with the Internal Revenue Code into those same waters. (We, quite patriotically, lifted it back out again for fear of polluting the water.) Thanks to the courageous deeds of those first Sons of Liberty we did not need to disguise ourselves in Mohawk Indian war paint and blankets, but the idea was the same. In our symbolic way, we were launching a new American revolution. We were beginning our quest to rid our country of an intolerable tax code and to return to Americans a capacity for determining their own future—a future free of the contradictory and oppressive instructions of a tax code that spells out in 5.5 million words how we are supposed to conduct our lives.

America's new Sons of Liberty look and sound quite different from that original band. Today they are the sons and daughters of American families who leave school to enter our increasingly insecure workforce and are indeed shocked to discover the total amount of taxes extracted from their first paycheck. They ask incredulously how and why their parents have put up with this unfair system of taxation for so long. They are also the American workers who watch as more and more good-paying jobs head for Mexico and the Far East. They are the American shoppers browsing through K-Mart and WalMart aisles littered with products made in China, Japan and Mexico. They are the small business owners spending, according to the Kemp Commission report, $4 in compliance costs for every $1 they eventually send to the U.S. Treasury in income taxes. They are the same small business owners or farmers concerned that they cannot pass on the business or family farm because of the inheritance tax bite.

They are the investors looking for the government-preferred investments rather than the investment that makes good business sense. And they are the citizens on April 15 struggling through the maze of the contradictory and confusing forms and regulations made necessary by a code that constantly changes both in form and interpretation. Most important, they are the citizens who work hard, play fair and attempt to raise their families with less than half their earned income, because government at some level has taken most of their income from them (often through withholdings they never see, or hidden taxes they aren't even aware of). They are the two-earner parents who spend less time with each other and with their children because one of them must work just to cover the family tax bills.

These new Sons and Daughters of Liberty are citizens who must take part in a new American Tea Party. Without their attendance, few in Washington will take this effort seriously, and we will all remain vassals to a freedom-eroding tax system.

TEA PARTIES DON'T HAPPEN IN WASHINGTON, D.C.

Washington, D.C., is heavily invested in the status quo—in the current system of income taxes that can and are regularly manipulated to benefit friends, punish enemies, reward political groups at the expense of others, and pursue the social policy goals of whatever political philosophy happens to be shared by those in power at any given time. True, there are some in Congress who have proposed to change things in a big way.

Congressman Bill Archer, the current chairman of the House Ways and Means Committee, has called upon the nation to "rip the income tax out by its roots." He is a true believer. He is as concerned as I am that the current U.S. income tax must go, and that we need a better and fairer tax system for our country. And Chairman Archer is in an ideal position to do something about it.

But here is the awful truth:

The effort will not succeed if it is left to Washington to make it happen. Why not? Simply put, Washington—the powers that be, the Congress itself, the political organizations, the Washington lobby—all are virtually beholden to the income tax code and its frequent revisions. A single statistic, I believe, makes the case.

In 1986, President Ronald Reagan gave us a law that, by its title alone, seemed to be the answer to many of our dreams: tax simplification. The law was The Tax Reform Act of 1986, and like every major IRS tax revision the need immediately arose for a "Technical Corrections Act." That meant hundreds of changes in the IRS code. Since 1986, the year of "tax simplification," tax bills enacted into law have provided us with over 4,700 changes to the income tax code. Imagine it—4,700 changes!

Many of those changes were minor, indeed technical. But some are significant.

5

They make a big difference to someone, or some group of people, or to American businesses. A lot of people worked hard to get those changes included in one bill or another. Some people were paid big commissions and bonuses for their help in lobbying those changes into law. The winners were very grateful. A lot of political purposes were served.

Many of those 4,700 changes make a big difference in the way Americans will work, spend, save, invest, or give to their favorite charity. Some of those changes will make a big difference in who gets support or opposition in the next political election cycle.

The income tax code is today the single most important instrument used in the hands of Washington politicians to exercise power over our lives. Think about it. It is the income tax code that makes one source of income excludable today and taxable tomorrow, that makes one expenditure deductible yesterday but not today, that diverts your savings toward one tax-preferred plan or another and your investment to this or that nontaxable investment. In fact, it is the income tax code that has established a new income redistribution plan for Americans in the guise of a "tax credit."

THE TAX CODE IS TOOL FOR SOCIAL ENGINEERING

Tax credits are usually thought of as a relief or return of taxes actually paid. Not so, anymore. The Earned Income Tax Credit (EITC) of our current income tax code is no credit at all. It does not represent a return of or relief from taxes paid or owed. The EITC is simply a U.S. government subsidy payment to an income earner who does not owe or pay a dime of U.S. income taxes because all of his income is exempt from taxation. That's right. The EITC is a transfer payment from real taxpayers to nonreal taxpayers (those who pay no income tax). It is a U.S. government program to share the wealth, a social program to subsidize low income earners with part of the earnings of real taxpayers. In short, it is a social welfare program designed as a tax credit.

The income tax code is also where the big political battles over class identification are played out, where we are separated into the *poor*, the *middle class*, and the *rich*. It is the focus of a read-my-lips presidential campaign pledge or another presidential promise to cut taxes for the middle class. It is the stage prop for the battle over Medicare reform. Congressional elections were fought over the question of whether some politicians really wanted to cut Medicare to give tax breaks to their wealthy friends or whether that was just "mediscare and medigoguery." U.S. income tax policy is at the heart of the balanced budget debate with some claiming that tax cuts and "corporate welfare" produce deficits while others argue for more tax cuts to drive down spending.

Here's the point I'm trying to make: The income tax code is at the center of everything that creates power in Washington. It is the fuel that drives the engine and the grease that lubricates the wheels. How and from where it is collected and to whom some of it is shared or distributed are the keys that unlock an understanding of how Washington works. Control these keys and you control the country.

If the IRS code is going to be repealed, the American people must do it. And if they do, they will become master again of their own fate. Government becomes the servant it was meant to be. People can take charge of their lives again. Taxpayers can become self-determinant. That is why folks at the power center in Washington will not yield control of these keys easily. They will use demagoguery, scare tactics, and misinformation to confuse the debate and destroy any chance of repeal. That is why America's new Sons and Daughters of Liberty must show up at the next American Tea Party and become part of the great grass roots movement to repeal the oppressive income tax code and abolish the dreaded IRS.

ABOARD THE BEAVER II, a replica of the original Boston Tea Party ship, Congressman Tauzin and his colleagues kicked off the tax reform movement that is sweeping the nation today. After the IRS code was thrown into Boston Harbor, it was immediately retrieved with ropes. "If we left it there," Congressman Tauzin told a cheering crowd, "we would be polluting Boston Harbor." (Photo by Frank Bordonaro)

"The IRS has become a symbol of the most intrusive, oppressive, and nondemocratic institution in our democratic society."

Former IRS Commissioner Fred Goldberg

CHAPTER 2

The Problem With Income Taxes

For most of the history of the United States, our country has funded its government operations through the imposition and collection of custom duties or tariffs on imported products, otherwise known as external taxes. Such a reliance on external taxes on foreign goods made abundant sense for a country struggling to catch up with the European world powers. Taxing imports rather than domestic products was a strategy that could easily be defended for a nation building itself out of a wilderness, still fulfilling its manifest destiny. Protectionist tariffs not only produced income from imports, they helped protect U.S. business and industry in those developmental years.

That's the way it was through most of the 19th century and into the early 20th century, right up to World War I. In fact, it seems that it was war—and the need to fund the weapons of war—that drove our country to look to internal taxes for new federal revenues to supplement the external income from tariffs.

Although the Civil War produced our nation's first income tax (the Lincoln tax was repealed at war's end), it was the years just preceding the U.S. entry into World War I that produced the Sixteenth Amendment in 1913 and the intolerable income tax under which we labor today.

What is even more remarkable is that a nation that depended for most of its existence on external taxes on imported products has most recently led the global economy away from protectionist tariffs and into the free-trading world of the General Agreement on Tariffs and Trade and the North American Free Trade Agreement. These agreements, and the rise of more and more open market communities and other open market trading agreements, predict even less reliance on external taxes around the world and here in the United States.

So we have succeeded in turning history upon its head; just like Alice walking through the looking glass.

We have gone from near-total dependence on import tariffs in one century, through another century of near-total dependence on income taxes. Now we're on the brink of a new millennium when tariffs are vanishing and income taxes appear to be our main source of income for the federal government. Are we willing to cross that proverbial bridge into the 21st century with income taxes as our principal support and with the IRS on our backs?

Is that a good idea? Is the U.S. income tax such a great idea that we ought to use it as the nearly exclusive source of national government funding? Is it the right tax policy in a global, free-trade society? Is the income tax a smart U.S. tax policy in the face of growing global competitiveness, where over 90 percent of American-made products now face foreign competition here in our own U.S. market?

To answer these questions we must look at the effect of the income tax on U.S. citizens, on the U.S. economy as a whole, and on U.S. import-export trade.

I start with these propositions:

> *(1) The U.S. income tax is an inefficient, overly complex and unfair set of laws that are inconsistent with a free people in a free economy.*

> *(2) The U.S. income tax is harmful to U.S. workers and manufacturers and to the U.S. economy as a whole.*

> *(3) The U.S. income tax encourages foreign imports and penalizes U.S. exports and is, thus, a bad idea in a free-trade, global society.*

WHY THE CODE IS COMPLEX AND UNFAIR

As stated earlier, the U.S. income tax laws, according to the Kemp Commission, force small businesses to pay $4 in compliance costs for every $1 sent to the U.S. Treasury. That's $4 of record keeping costs, accounting costs, filling out forms and tax audits and appeals. In addition, the American public spends approximately $300 billion worth of man-hours to properly account for and complete our personal income tax forms. That's a mind-boggling 5.5 billion hours.

When you read or hear about the inefficiency of the IRS collection system, take note that the IRS only counts its own costs, not those of U.S. citizens who "voluntarily" do most of the work. Remember, the IRS audits less than two percent of returns filed. Americans, who are charged under the system of being capable of proving they are honest

10

and accurate, do most of the work and bear the burden of most of the costs. Also, take note of these little tidbits of information:

✔ The IRS annually spends more than $10 billion and employs five times as many people as the FBI and twice as many as the CIA.

✔ The IRS recently lost 4,600 computer tapes containing the records of thousands of U.S. taxpayers.

✔ The IRS recently disciplined numerous employees and dismissed some for the unthinkable—illegally snooping into citizens "confidential" tax forms.

✔ The IRS, according to former employees, trained its employees to resent U.S. citizens for their earnings and their lifestyles, and regularly destroys its records to insure no one ever discovers its inner workings.

✔ From 1954 to 1994, the number of words in the income tax code increased to more than 800,000 from less than 200,000.

✔ U.S. citizens fill out 308 million tax forms a year—at an average cost of $256 per form (which amounts to a 15 percent surtax levied on all federal receipts).

✔ Even the 1040 EZ form takes an estimated 2.9 hours to fill out at an approximate cost of $122.

✔ The IRS "gotcha" mind-set even extends to its tactics in the field, such as raids on restaurants and homes with drawn guns, as happened to two Virginia restaurants. After tearing the businesses apart, some (but only some) of the files were ultimately returned with the curt note: "The investigation is over. There will be no charges." The IRS is immune by law from legal action.

✔ "States that have a flatter, simpler income tax system—or perhaps no income tax at all—are far out pacing other states in personal income, economic growth and job creation," according to economists J. Kenneth Blackwell and Richard Vedder.

THE PROBLEM WITH INCOME TAXES

✔ Personal income per capita rose more than 40 percent faster in Texas and Florida during the last business cycle through the third quarter of 1996, than it did in California. Texas and Florida, not coincidentally, have no state income taxes.

✔ The poorer-performing states all have highly progressive income tax levies.

✔ Not surprisingly, people move from high-tax to flat-rate states. From 1990 to 1995, the nation's 16 flat-rate income tax states, had net immigration of native-born Americans of 181,000—about 1,000 each business day. All of them were fleeing from progressive income tax states.

✔ The experience of the states suggests to many researchers that moving to a saner, fairer, growth-oriented tax system would significantly boost American real output from its current long-run rate—a historically low 2.5 percent a year. It would also remove millions from the tax rolls while making all those remaining play by the same simple rules.

CONGRESSMAN TAUZIN, flanked by more than 100 of his colleagues, including Majority Leader Dick Armey and Speaker Newt Gingrich, announced the "Scrap the Code" tour during a rally at the U.S. Capitol. Millions of Americans have seen the Tauzin-Armey debates either in person or on television. (Photo by Steve Rusnik)

"In principle, the income tax, at this time, is incompatible with freedom."

Ambassador Alan Keyes

CHAPTER 3

Guilty! The IRS On Trial

During an audit, the Internal Revenue Service assumes you're guilty. Beware: It's up to you to prove your innocence. You may be as honest as the day is long. You may even be believable. But if you do not have the satisfactory records and receipts to back up your return, you cannot establish your innocence, and the presumption of guilt will prevail. You get a better deal than that in any federal court—even after indictment by a federal grand jury. In court, you are innocent and remain so until and unless a trial by your peers finds otherwise. With the IRS, the ordinary constitutional protections are turned on their head. Instead of government of, by, and for the people, the IRS has become the judge, jury, and executioner.

While room 219 of the Dirksen Senate Office Building in Washington, D.C., is not a courtroom, for one week in late September, 1997, it could have been. There, before the glare of television lights, the mighty IRS faced the people of the United States represented by members of the U.S. Senate Finance Committee. The tables were turned. The IRS literally found itself on trial. Accused of intentionally violating the rights of ordinary citizens in one horror story after another, acting IRS Commissioner Michael P. Dolan did the unthinkable. He pleaded guilty. Then came this landmark apology:

> *"No one should have endured what these citizens describe as their experiences at the hand of the tax system. At this point, I offer my sincere apology to these taxpayers for any mistakes we have made and for any anguish we have caused."*

What he did not offer was the never-to-be-heard apology for a tax system that created an agency like the IRS and empowered it to abuse the people of our country.

We did hear from some of the victims. We did hear from former IRS employees, who testified behind screens with disguised voices about how they abused American citizens.

HORROR STORIES ABOUND

Monsignor Lawrence Ballweg told how the IRS—because of a simple name error—threatened to seize his bank account, auto, and other property because of an $18,000 tax lien which he did not owe.

Then there was the case of Katherine Lund Hicks of Apple Valley, California, who settled her tax dispute (involving a former marriage) with the IRS and paid the settlement only to have her property and that of her new husband seized. Forced to divorce her new husband to avoid the tax liens, which the IRS later acknowledged never should have been filed, she was pursued by the IRS for over a decade seeking money she did not owe. At one point, she tried to pay them, only to be rebuffed by the IRS. "For over 10 years," she tearfully told the committee, "the IRS conducted itself as a legalized extortion operation....The IRS is answerable to none." The result was predictable. "My credit is completely destroyed, and my husband's credit is seriously damaged. We will suffer the effects of the IRS collection for the rest of our lives."

Next up was Tom Savage of Lewes, Delaware, who was the victim of an IRS decision to fabricate a partnership agreement between his company and one of his subcontractors (who was tax delinquent). Pointing to this bogus partnership, the IRS seized $14,000 of his income. Unable to pay his bills, he settled with the IRS for $50,000, which he did not owe. Speaking of the criminal acts committed by an IRS agent, Savage told the committee: "He created a company that did not exist." Amazingly, the committee produced an internal memo from the Justice Department to the IRS district counsel to the effect that the agency had no case against Savage. They intentionally defrauded him out of $50,000 and fabricated documents to do so. If anyone else did that sort of thing, the Justice Department would haul them before a grand jury.

VULNERABLE TAXPAYERS TARGETED

One of the IRS employees speaking anonymously to the Senate Finance Committee explained it: "The IRS protects itself, whether right or wrong." Another IRS agent, Jennifer Long, put it more bluntly. She told the Finance Committee how her colleagues falsify evidence to extract money from taxpayers and in the process "ruin families' lives and businesses." She said: "I have actually witnessed IRS management manipulate income tax return figures just to increase their office or district collection statistics." Agent Long may have summarized the whole sad mess when she commented, "Under present IRS management it is now our job to 'stick it' to the taxpayers."

To which taxpayers? Senate Finance Committee Chairman William V. Roth, Jr., left no doubt about the answer to that question. His six-month investigation had convinced him that IRS agents were targeting lower-and-middle-income taxpayers, "who can't afford to fight back."

Later in the hearings, IRS Agent Long confirmed that the agency was after the most vulnerable taxpayers, specifically poorer taxpayers with limited understanding of their legal rights. She insisted, despite IRS claims, that agents are encouraged to make up tax assessments and go after those poorer taxpayers. And if they fight back? "God help the taxpayer!" she responded. As of late, she continued, "We seem to be auditing only poor people."

"These have been very painful days," acting IRS Commissioner Dolan admitted. "Painful because it distresses me greatly the mistakes we've made, to see the impact of those mistakes."

But were they mistakes? Or are they the kind of behavior expected of an agency drunk with power, with a right to declare any American citizen guilty and then pursue the victim like a hound from hell until he or she either surrenders or is able to prove their own innocence? Even then, even after all of the anguish, accounting and legal fees, even after establishing your innocence, there is still a mess to be cleaned up...getting the tax liens removed and all the credit records corrected and reestablished. Do you think the IRS will be anxious to help you re-establish your credit and remove the liens? Guess again!

IRS AGENTS FATTEN BATTING AVERAGES

Part of the reason for the IRS's exuberant excesses has been the practice, according to Senator Roth, of levying tax assessments "simply [to] raise [the] individual statistics of an IRS employee," and, therefore, indirectly furthering the practice of using tax collection quotas to rate agents or officers.

Newsweek magazine reported, in its October 6, 1997, edition, that it obtained an August 4 memorandum from Arkansas/Oklahoma IRS district collection chief Ronald James, which details just such a system, where agents are evaluated by the number of seizures, liens, and levies. Immediately after the Senate hearings, Dolan issued an order to stop using such data to rate the IRS districts, thus confirming the practice actually occurred.

As a result of the hearings, the IRS has come under increased attention and investigative reporting. *Newsweek,* in particular, featured an October 13, 1997 cover story by reporter Michael Hirsch, which follows a major feature on the congressional hearings in its previous issue.

Hirsch's report on the hearings contains the following summary of the witness testimony: "They told of an IRS that is a virtual police state within a democracy, a B--- like fiefdom of tax terror at the heart of the U.S. economy."

The IRS, witnesses said, is almost never held accountable for its many errors and sins. It is an agency that audits people on a supervisor's whim, frames taxpayers with false claims, seizes property and places liens illegally, and retaliates against anyone it pleases, including tax protestors. In one case, they went as far as auditing a critic who wrote a letter to the editor.

Hirsch quoted a Finance Committee spokesman: "All the committee phones lit up." Hirsch went on to write:

> "*If the true number of incidences of taxpayer abuse were ever known, the public would be appalled,' said one witness, a former IRS collection agent. 'If the public also ever knew [how much is] covered up by the IRS, there could be a tax revolt.'*"

Hirsch, in another *Newsweek* cover story, began to uncover some of those IRS secrets in an investigative report on the Arkansas/Oklahoma IRS district. In his expose', Hirsch reports that Larry Lakey, a revenue officer who worked with district director Ronald James—who is currently under suspension—told how James "would just come right out and tell us that our evaluations would be based on the number of seizures we did," adding that nonperformers were forced out.

OTHER SHOCKING STORIES EMERGE

It gets worse. A lawyer, Donald Heller of Miami, Florida, represented a newspaper that ran a 1973 expose' of an illegal IRS spying operation. IRS agents demanded he give up his sources; he refused. As a result, he was investigated, indicted and convicted in 1982 and finally imprisoned in 1983. The U.S. Court of Appeals later found that he had been framed by the IRS agents, who had presumed his own accountant to be under oath. Freed, Mr. Heller collected $5 million from his accountant's insurance company and $500,000 from the IRS. He gave the IRS settlement to charity.

If false management were not bad enough, consider the case of Alex and Kay

Council. Several years ago, the IRS was pursuing a $300,000 tax lien against the couple. One day, Kay Council found this note on the family kitchen table: **"I have taken my life in order to provide capital for you. The IRS and its liens taken against our property illegally by a runaway agency of our government have dried up all the sources of credit for us. So I have made the only decision I can. I hope you can understand that. I love you completely. Alex."**

Sadly, Alex Council took his life. His wife collected $250,000 from an insurance company and continued to fight the IRS in court. Eventually she won. A federal judge ordered the IRS to repay her nearly $30,000 for attorney fees and expenses and to immediately drop its "wrongful" case against her. She won a court victory, but lost her husband.

So there you have it—a federal agency that can declare you guilty, seize your assets, lien your property and pursue you to your grave; an agency that apparently thinks it's appropriate behavior to falsify documents (fabricating them out of the air when necessary), pressure witnesses to lie, deny citizens the chance to prove their innocence; an agency that encourages its agents to phony up tax assessments against citizens to meet goals and statistical quotas; and an agency that often targets the most vulnerable in our society—the poor-and-middle-income taxpayers, who cannot afford to fight back or do not know how.

Why do we tolerate such a government agency in a free country such as ours? Why have we allowed the kind of IRS abuses disclosed in the Senate hearings to go on for so long? Is it the fault of the IRS management? The Treasury Department? The White House? Congress?

President Clinton reacted to the Senate hearings with a call for a citizen review board—a watchdog agency to help police the IRS. But is this an admission that the Administration has not, or cannot, do its job of managing the IRS? Or is it an admission of something even more profound? Is the problem bigger than any Administration? Is it a problem with the very institution of the income tax system and the IRS?

The biggest fault of all, according to Stephen Moore, a budget analyst at the CATO Institute, lies with the body that has the power to correct it once and for all, the U.S. Congress. "The villain here," Mr. Moore told the Associated Press, "is Congress, because the IRS has a hopeless task to administer and enforce a tax code that is ultimately unenforceable."

As awful as the IRS enforcement may be, I submit, as did Moore, that it is what the income tax does, more than how it is enforced, which inflicts the most serious harm to the citizens it is supposed to serve.

AMERICAN FREEDOM UNDERMINED BY IRS

Free people in a free society founded and structured on the principles of private property and free markets are best served by a tax system that respects and enlarges upon these freedoms. The income tax code is designed to do the opposite—to constantly restrict and confine those freedoms. It has served to enlarge the center of power in our country, Washington, D.C., and then to corrupt that power.

Free people in a free-market system depend in large part upon the degree of interference they experience from their government. Granted, government's main task is to protect our freedoms, but it also regularly interferes. That interference may be in the form of unnecessary regulation or restrictions upon our activities, but it may also come in the guise of "help" or "stimulation" (as in a new tax-stimulus package). Make no mistake—it is interference. For when the government decides to help or stimulate, it conversely decides what to hinder or discourage. And what is "given" today is more often than not "taken away" tomorrow—often retroactively. Just ask every passive investor who witnessed the tax reform of 1986, which retroactively eliminated the former tax policy of helping investors with a passive-loss deduction.

Each government income tax decision may have one of many different purposes: Either to raise more revenue; to encourage one economic activity or to discourage another; to reward one set of friends (special interests) or to punish another; to play to one economic class (rich, poor, middle class) at the expense of another; or, perhaps, to influence some behavior, such as preventing development that is disliked by the environmental community, or encouraging so-called "green" activities. For good, or not so good motives, income tax decisions interfere with our lives. They tell us how to earn our income (which income is tax preferred); how to spend our income (which spending is tax deductible); how to save our income (which forms of savings are taxable and which are not); how to invest our earnings (which investments, for example, are tax free, which are subject to capital gains taxes); how to give our money away (which gifts are deductible and which are not); how to plan our retirements (which pensions are taxable and which are not); how to treat our children during our lives (which gifts to our children are subject to gift taxes and which are not); and how to leave our assets to our heirs at death (what property is subject to inheritance tax if we chose to leave it to a particular person). Is this interference or not? Do such decisions enlarge or restrict the freedoms of otherwise free people?

Income tax interference with freedom gets even more obnoxious as the number of such tax provisions increase in number and importance. The income tax code and regulations now comprise over 17,000 pages with 5.5 million words. Every page and every one of those millions of words represent decisions that interfere in our lives. And the changes come fast and furious.

Since 1986, when President Ronald Reagan gave us tax simplification, Congress has, in its infinite wisdom, returned the favor with a mere 4,700 changes in the income tax code. Each change, big or small, has affected some citizen's life. Each change has limited some citizen or group of citizens in the free exercise of their financial and economic life. Each change, for good or evil motives, defines the boundaries of our freedoms.

TAX POLICY DICTATES OUR LIVES

What is it about Congress that produces such volumes of tax-policy changes almost every year? Does this power to easily interfere in our daily lives help or hinder the integrity of the institution?

Campaign finance reform is the hot topic of the day. Admittedly, too much money flows in from too many questionable sources, creating the impression that we have the best federal government money can buy. Is it any wonder that less than 50 percent of the American public even bothered to vote in the presidential election of 1996? Granted, there are many reasons for such a low and diminishing voter turnout rate, but cynicism clearly plays a major role.

Because Congress has so much power over the future of every American, every business enterprise, every social institution and, literally, all aspects of the nation's economy, Congress is a heavily courted institution. Double that for those members of Congress who can make a difference in tax policy: Members of the Ways and Means Committee in the House; the Senate Finance Committee; the House and Senate Rules Committee; and the House and Senate leadership.

Look hard at the income tax code, with all its power to affect what each one of us does or does not do with his money, and you are looking into the heart of power in Washington, D.C. If Joseph Conrad were seeking the *Heart of Darkness* of the American political experience, he would certainly find it in room 1100 of the Longworth House Office Building (where the House Ways and Means Committee meets) and room 229 of the Dirksen Senate Office Building (where the Senate Finance Committee meets).

This is not to speak unkindly of the hardworking men and women duly elected to serve in the Congress and selected to serve on those two key tax-writing committees. It is the nature of the beast. Give Congress and these two committees such power and you must expect it will be used, and that every special interest will attempt to influence the exercise of that power to their advantage. That is simply not healthy.

Perhaps the best medicine we could administer to the disease of political money that is believed to corrupt our system would be to remove from Congress such pervasive power over the economic decisions made by a people who still cherish freedom and yearn for more, not less of it. Repealing the income tax would do wonders for our nation's political health. Repealing the income tax would dramatically curtail the power that Washington has over our lives, dramatically expand our freedoms, and dramatically increase our personal ability to pursue the happiness that our forefathers predicted for us when they put their own lives, freedoms, and futures on the line for the sake of ours.

INCOME TAX IS HARMFUL TO U.S. ECONOMY

The power to tax has been described as the power to destroy. Tax something and you discourage it. Tax it more and you destroy it. Taxes can be designed to send specific messages: What is encouraged and what is not encouraged in society. It is useful, therefore, to look at the message our income tax code sends.

The current code taxes the production of income; it taxes interest on our savings accounts; it taxes gains on our investments; it taxes gifts we give to our children (through the gift tax); and it taxes legacies for our children (through the death tax). Most perversely, it taxes the production of products and services "made in America" with a complex income tax that costs $300 billion a year to comply with. What kind of message does that send?

Our income tax code punishes you for earning income, punishes you for saving, punishes you for investing, punishes you for giving to your children in life or in death, and punishes you when you buy anything made in America. It rewards you (by not taxing you) only when you buy imported products. Are those good messages for the U.S. economy? Are those good messages for the U.S. laborer? Is making something in America considered by our government and its tax code as a bad activity, while importing something made in some other country a good activity? Isn't there something wrong here? Have the inmates taken over the insane asylum?

Assume that you live in a country that is facing increased competition from other industrialized and industrializing nations. Your country's savings rate is notoriously low while the personal savings rate of your competitor economies range from 12 percent to 28 percent of disposable income. Would you want a government tax policy that favors savings or discourages savings?

Assume that your country has a historic gross national product growth of 2.5-to-3.5 percent, and your competing economies are experiencing growth rates double and triple yours. Would you favor a tax code that discouraged investment by taxing capital gains, or would you see the wisdom of encouraging capital gains and investments in production?

Assume that the balance of trade with competing economies continues to be negative ($100 billion-plus a year) because your country imports more foreign products than your country exports to foreign countries. Assume your trade imbalance now ranges from $100-to-$150 billion per year and that every $1 billion costs you about 19,000 American jobs. Would you want an income tax with expensive compliance costs that affect U.S. production, while reducing and eliminating tariffs on imported products? Would you be concerned enough about trade deficits, job losses and job insecurity, to be willing to re-examine your country's tax policy? I should hope so.

TAX CODE PUNISHES AMERICAN WORKERS

An income tax policy designed in an age of protectionist tariffs, or fashioned during a period of U.S. trade surpluses was one thing. To continue an income tax policy that effectively taxes only the products of American labor while permitting foreign imports to enter our marketplace—totally or partially tax exempt—is quite another. Every American worker who is fortunate enough to earn a decent living, despite the punishing effect of income taxes withheld from his paycheck, should be outraged to know that when he spends his after-tax dollars on American goods and services he gets taxed again, but when he spends those same dollars on foreign imported products he does not get taxed again. What's worse, fellow Americans are discouraged from buying products resulting from his effort by an income tax code that taxes only domestic businesses. When did we come to disrespect American labor so that we treat the products and labor of our foreign competitors so much better?

What's the answer? Let's repeal the income tax code and replace it with a tax code that no longer punishes American labor and income, that no longer punishes savings and investments and that taxes foreign imported products at the same rate it taxes American made products. Common sense tells us that to keep the current income tax code in the face of these challenging times and free trade agreements is not just foolish, it's economically insane.

When presidential candidate Pat Buchanan was barnstorming across the country during the 1996 Republican primary season, stirring the "peasants with pitchforks" to rise up against the job losses produced by free-trade agreements such as NAFTA and GATT, he was striking a real chord of American awareness. Unfortunately, he chose the wrong culprit. It is not free trade that is the enemy of the U.S. laborer, it is our own oppressive income tax code, which taxes only American products and labor. We need to get rid of this discriminating income tax code and replace it with a border-adjustable tax—a tax that equally taxes foreign imports and American-made products. Then GATT and NAFTA would make a lot more sense.

TAX CODE ENCOURAGES FOREIGN IMPORTS

Because our system taxes only American business income (with both taxes and compliance costs) it places a double whammy on U.S. products and labor, here in the U.S. market and again in every U.S. export market.

In our own market, the discriminating effect of the income tax code is particularly evident. Foreign products not subject to income taxes have a clear advantage. But it is an advantage that is compounded by the fact that many of our free-trading partners have border-adjustable taxes, like the VAT (Value-Added Tax). These border-adjustable taxes are collected at home in the foreign country when homegrown products are purchased there by that country's citizens. The trick is that those border-adjustable taxes are not collected (rebated) on products sold to others or exported from that foreign country.

So the foreign product enters the U.S. market without having to pay the foreign VAT tax and without paying U.S. income taxes. It's a pretty good deal and is all permitted under GATT.

TAX CODE PENALIZES AMERICAN EXPORTS

In the foreign market, the effect is much the same. There, the U.S. product, carrying the full weight of American income taxes on its back, arrives in the foreign market and is slapped with a VAT tax. The domestic product in the foreign market also pays the local VAT tax, but it does not carry the huge cost of the American tax code and the compliance cost that is carried by the U.S. product.

Any wonder that we have a huge trade deficit? It's remarkable that it isn't worse.

What is also remarkable is that we could enter agreements like GATT—which permit border-adjustable taxes—without recognizing our import-export handicap, when other countries take advantage of border-adjustability and we do not.

In my opinion, the single best thing we could do to end our trade deficits, to increase the market power of American-made products, both here and abroad, would be to repeal the income tax code and replace it with a simple, border-adjustable tax.

In the following chapters, I will elaborate on the inequities of the current income tax code and describe a sensible plan to replace it with a 15 percent national retail sales tax. I will also describe our effort in Congress and what you must do to make it all happen.

IN DEBATES around the nation, Congressman Tauzin called the IRS code "oppressive and mean-spirited." In 1998, he pointed out that Americans will pay more in taxes than they do for food, clothing and shelter combined. Put another way, every dollar you earn between January and May will go to pay taxes—every penny of it. (Photo by Paul Grounds)

"The income tax has made liars out of more Americans than even golf."

Will Rogers

CHAPTER 4

"This Bed Was Burning When We Got Into It"
(A Brief History Of The American Income Tax)

We didn't get into this mess easily. The American income tax has experienced a rather sordid history. It has been through enactment, then repeal; constitutional challenges, then rejection; Constitutional Amendment, countless simplification complications, reforms, and revisions. We have seen rates as high as 90 percent (1960) and as low as one percent (1913). The IRS code has grown from two short pages in 1913 to a code of 800,000 words, not to mention the 6,439 pages of regulations.

April 15, once nothing more than a beautiful springtime day in our lives, has become a day we approach with fear and trepidation, the day the tax man cometh.

The Tax Man.

How did we invent him and why?

Somehow, some way, our great country managed to run itself quite well without a federal income tax for 132 of our 230 years of existence—from 1776 to 1861 and again from 1872 to 1913.

All during this time, we funded the federal government primarily through taxes (or tariffs) on foreign imports. Taxes on foreign goods were known as external taxes to distinguish them from taxes on domestic products, or internal taxes.

Two early attempts at internal taxation were short-lived. From 1791 to 1802, pursuant to the Reserve Act of March 3, 1791, and subsequent amendments, internal taxes were levied on distilled spirits, carriages, refined sugar, snuff, property sold at auction, bonds, and legal instruments. Those taxes produced such vehement opposition that the 1794 Whiskey Rebellion in Pennsylvania resulted. In 1798, direct taxes on real property were added, complete with assessment districts, appointed assessors, and the necessary regulations for the valuation of lands and improvements and even the enumeration of slaves.

Thomas Jefferson put an end to all that in 1802, abolishing the tax system and all 400 revenue jobs. The country again relied on external taxes, tariffs, and other customs duties on foreign imports.

In 1813, with the costs of the War of 1812 confronting the nation, Congress passed the Revenue Act of July 24, 1813. Taxes were levied again on distillers and carriages, refined sugar and sales at auction. Within a short time, taxes were added on retail liquor dealers, retailers of imported products, bank notes, legal instruments, distilled spirits, domestically manufactured products, household furniture, watches, gold, silver and jewelry.

Then, with the War of 1812 behind them, Congress, in 1815, abolished all those internal taxes and the revenue jobs that went with them.

Except for those two short periods, our country managed to pay the cost of its national government exclusively with customs duties, that is, until 1861—the beginning of the American Civil War. And even during and after that war, it was not until 1900 that internal taxes equaled, and eventually exceeded, the amounts collected by customs duties. There's the irony. Our country, born in a tax rebellion in Boston Harbor, survived for over half of its life on taxes levied principally on foreign goods imported into our country.

Since 1900, and especially since the birth of our current income tax system, we have reversed that equation. Today we tax every endeavor, every product made in America, and more and more we extend free trade to foreign-made products. No wonder jobs are leaving our country. No wonder we suffer from a continuing trade deficit. No wonder we've become the world's premier debtor nation. Understanding how we got into this mess is critical to finding our way out.

HISTORY OF AMERICAN INCOME TAXES

Our first experience with an income tax began with the coming of the Civil War. The Civil War Revenue Act of August 5, 1861, authorized America's first income tax. The 1861 act and the Revenue Act of 1862 taxed a broad variety of products, including income. The 1862 act created a new Office of the Commissioner of Internal Revenue under the Secretary of the Treasury, and created 185 collection districts with an appointed assessor and collector for each district. The Act further created civil and criminal prosecutions as its chief enforcement mechanisms. Though many of the early activities were associated with liquor tax collections, the system was understandably rife with abuse. Collectors and their deputies, for example, were paid on a commission rather than a salary basis. Inspectors were paid fees by the manufacturers they inspected. George S. Bartwell of Massachusetts was appointed the first Commissioner of the Internal Revenue.

Shortly thereafter, new taxes were added, including the first inheritance tax. In 1865, Congress created its first commission to study abuses in the tax system it created, although the study focused primarily on patronage issues. Congress responded with—you guessed it—more patronage and more bureaucracy; more deputies; a solicitor; seven heads of divisions; new clerks; messengers; and laborers. In short, more headaches for Americans.

Thankfully, the Civil War ended and Congress began to disband the system. In 1867, the progressive rate structure of the income tax was abolished. Washington temporarily bought into a flat tax argument. Then, in 1872, Congress got religion and repealed the entire income tax. In 1879, Congress followed up by repealing the inheritance tax.

Income taxes were not heard from again until 1894. For more than two decades, Congress was kept busy trying to enforce even higher taxes on liquor that produced escalating levels of corruption and violence. Between 1876 and 1880, nearly 100 federal tax agents were killed or wounded.

Congress then turned its attention to special interest and regulatory taxation in 1886, taxing oleomargarine to protect butter, and in 1890, taxing U.S. opium to discourage its manufacture. While these and other taxes on child labor and foreign labor were true revenue measures, they represented the first real effort by Congress at social engineering through taxation, a feature heavily present in the current income tax system.

INCOME TAXES, LIKE OLD HABITS, DIE HARD

In 1894, Congress got the income tax bug again. Tucked away somewhere deep in the Wilson Tariff Act of 1894, Congress for the second time authorized a progressive income tax. Fortunately, the Constitution of the United States rode to the rescue.

The 1894 Income Tax Act imposed a federal income tax on:

"The gain, profits, and income received in the preceding calendar year by every

citizen of the United States .... whether said gains, profits, or income be derived from any kind of property, rents, interest, dividends, or salaries, or from any profession, trade, employment, or vocation carried on in the United States or elsewhere...."

A challenge to this Act reached the U.S. Supreme Court in the landmark case of **Pollack v. Farmers Loan and Trust Company** (157 U.S. 429, rehearing 158 U.S. 601, 1895).

In that decision, the Supreme Court was asked to interpret that statute in light of Article 1, Section 9, Clause 4 of the Constitution, which states:

"No Capitation, or other direct Tax shall be laid, unless in proportion to the Census of Enumeration herein before directed to be taken."

The Court was also asked to rule on Article 1, Section 8, Clause 1 of the Constitution, which states:

"The Congress shall have the power to lay and collect Taxes, Duties and Excises, to pay the Debts and provide for the Common Defense and general Welfare of the United States; but all Duties, Imports and Excises shall be uniform throughout the United States."

To understand the Supreme Court's eventual decision, it is important to understand the difference between direct and indirect taxes. Direct taxes, covered by Article 1, Section 9, Clause 4 had to be in "proportion to the Census of Enumeration." Indirect taxes, by Article 1, Section 8, Clause 1, are subject to the requirement that they be "uniform throughout the United States."

Direct taxes are of two types—taxes on property (real and personal) and capitation taxes (head taxes). Both had to be levied in "proportion to the Census...." For example, in 1813, Congress passed such a direct property tax apportioned among the then 18 states and among the counties (parishes) of each state (Act of August 2, 1813, 2 Stat. 53). Congress has never enacted a so-called "head tax."

All other taxes (not direct as described above) are considered indirect and, thus, subject to the rule of uniformity; that is, that they not discriminate geographically, such as an income tax imposed on the citizens of only one state (United States v. Ptasynski, 462 U.S. 74, 1983).

30

In the **Pollack** decision, the Supreme Court struck down the entire Income Tax Act of 1894. But here's the most important part of the decision: The Supreme Court did not find unconstitutional the income tax provisions of the Act that taxed *"gains, profits or incomes...derived from...salaries or from any profession, trade, employment or vocation...."*

The Supreme Court simply ruled that the income tax on the gains derived from investments on real or personal property was unconstitutional (because those taxes were considered direct on property), and because those direct taxes had not been apportioned among the states.

In this respect, the 1894 tax would have been valid to the extent that it imposed income taxes on the "gains, profits, or income...derived from...salaries, or from any profession, trade, employment, or vocation...."

The Court struck down the entire 1894 Act (on rehearing) only because it believed that to strike down a part of the Act (the income taxes on property gains) and to leave the rest (the income taxes on salaries, etc.) in place would be contrary to congressional intent.

The important conclusion which must be drawn from the **Pollack** decision is most profound and contrary to popular belief:

> *The Supreme Court never ruled the income tax on salaries was unconstitutional. The Sixteenth Amendment of 1913 was required only to make constitutional the income tax on capital gains.*

With or without the Sixteenth Amendment, Congress can constitutionally enact an income tax on personal and business income (as long as it does not contain a tax on capital gains or other property earnings).

Therefore, repealing the Sixteenth Amendment would only prevent Congress from taxing the gains derived from investment on real or personal property. Even then, Congress would not be constitutionally prevented from imposing income taxes on such "capital gains" as long as those taxes were apportioned among the states on the basis of the last census.

In 1913, with the prospect of America's involvement in the great World War, Congress proposed, and the states ratified, the Sixteenth Amendment to the Constitution which provided that:

> *"The Congress shall have the power to lay and collect taxes on income, from whatever sources derived, without apportionment among the several States, and without regard to any census or enumeration."*

The amendment, simply put, made it clear that income taxes—even those on income derived from property investments—would be legal, without having to be apportioned among the states on the basis of the last census.

Congress quickly responded with the passage of another federal income tax substantially similar to the 1894 tax (38 Stat. 166). The 1913 tax was imposed on:

> *"Gains, profits, and income derived from salaries, wages, or compensation for personal service of whatever kind and in whatever form paid, or from professions, vocations, businesses, trade, commerce, or sales, or dealings in property whether real or personal, growing out of the ownership or use of or interest in real or personal property, also from interest, rent, dividends, securities, or the transactions of any lawful business carried on for gain or profit, or gains or profits and income derived from any sources whatsoever, including the income from but not the value of property acquired by gift, bequest, devises or descent."*

In 1916, in a case entitled **Brushaber v. Union Pacific Railroad Company**, the Supreme Court reviewed the 1913 tax law and found that it was constitutional in its entirety.

Most important, the Supreme Court found again that the inherent character of our income tax was that of an "indirect" tax; that the Sixteenth Amendment did not authorize any new type of tax, nor did it repeal or revise the tax clauses of Article 1. The Supreme Court found that the Sixteenth Amendment only made it clear that an income tax would not be considered a direct tax even when it applied to income derived from property investments.

The obvious conclusion, again, is that income taxes on salaries and business incomes are and were constitutional with or without the Sixteenth Amendment. Simply repealing the Sixteenth Amendment will not change that fact.

Much has been made of the fact that the ratification resolution passed by a number of states contained variations from the resolution enacted by Congress in punctuation, capitalization, and/or spelling. Some have claimed that the U.S. income tax is invalid because the Sixteenth Amendment was not properly ratified and, thus, not part of the

Constitution.

There are three problems with this argument:

First, the income tax, with or without the Sixteenth Amendment, has never been declared unconstitutional. As pointed out earlier, the 1895 decision only declared unconstitutional the tax on income derived from property because Congress failed to apportion that tax among the states.

Second, the 1913 Act was specifically declared constitutional; and

Third, Secretary of State Philander C. Knox in 1913 certified adoption of the Sixteenth Amendment pursuant to section 205 of the revised statutes of the United States (current version at 1 U.S.C. § 106b). In the Supreme Court case of **Leser v. Garnett**, the Court was faced with a case very nearly directly on point: A challenge to the Sixteenth Amendment on the basis that two states (Tennessee and West Virginia) had improperly adopted their resolutions of ratification. In that decision, the Court ruled that "official notice to the Secretary, duly authenticated, that they had [adopted the resolution of ratification] was conclusive upon him, and, being certified by his proclamation, is conclusive upon the courts."(**Leser v. Garnett**, 258 U.S. 130, 1922).

Several Courts of Appeals in various circuits have specifically considered the question of the certification by Secretary Knox and the ratification of the Sixteenth Amendment. In every case, the Courts have ruled that certification by Secretary Knox in 1913 is conclusive upon the Courts, and, therefore, the Sixteenth Amendment is considered part of the U.S. Constitution.

It should be noted that in both the 7th Circuit and the 9th Circuit cases, writs to the Supreme Court were applied for and were denied. The usual interpretation of such denial of writs is that the Supreme Court agrees with the Court of Appeals' decision.

Thus, the Sixteenth Amendment stands, and even without the Amendment, so would the income tax, at least insofar as it applies to salaried and business income.

That said, our first code began so modestly, so reasonably, that it is hard to believe that it has morphed into the monster that taxpayers face today. It began as a tax of one percent on the net personal income over $3,000 and a surtax of six percent on income over $500,000. The act repealed the constitutionally questionable corporation tax of 1909 and relieved a net corporate income tax of one percent on income in excess of $5,000. The 1913 Income Tax Act was not only the foundation for our current system, it also provides the first system of collection through withholding of the source of income, in itself a very controversial concept. By 1916, the withholding provision proved to be politically difficult, and it was repealed. Nineteen years later, the Social Security Act was adopted and that 1935 Act became the authority to withhold taxes from income, an authority which, of course, survives today. Field auditing became an active feature of the system by 1920. Decentralized management, which has led to regional offices rendering different interpretations of code provisions and IRS regulations also was well established by 1920.

The rest is a history of revisions, reform, enlargement and growth, resulting in the extraordinarily complex, confusing and unfair code we endure today.

THE PRESENT TAX SYSTEM TAXES OUR MONEY

TWICE!

AMERICANS ARE TAXED BOTH COMING AND GOING

PERSONAL INCOME

...ON INCOME TAXES
WITHHELD
FROM
PAYCHECKS

PERSONAL CONSUMPTION

...ON HIDDEN
BUSINESS TAXES
ADDED TO THE COST
OF OUR PURCHASES

...THROUGH GIFTS AND
INHERITANCE TAXES
IF WE DON'T SPEND IT

ONCE IS ENOUGH!

"TAX REFORM isn't just about money," Congressman Tauzin told enthusiastic supporters during a recent rally, "it's also about freedom in America." Today the IRS is bigger than both the CIA and FBI combined. In other words, Tauzin added, "we spend more money tracking down taxpayers than we do terrorists." (Photo by Frank Bordonaro)

"I want to get back to an America free from the IRS."

House Speaker Newt Gingrich

CHAPTER 5

"Double-Double, Toil And Trouble"
(Conversation With An American Businessman)

The IRS income tax is a double-taxation system, taxing most of us twice on the same money we earn. You don't believe me? I'll prove it to you.

How many of you believe that businesses in America actually pay income taxes? If you do, you're wrong for the most part.

Every time I sit next to a businessman on the two-hour-plus plane ride from Washington, D.C., to my district in Louisiana, I engage him in a discussion that goes pretty much like this:

Tauzin: Do you believe that businesses pay taxes in America?

Businessman: Of course we pay taxes. We pay lots of taxes.

Tauzin: Wrong.

Businessman: What do you mean wrong? I'm telling you we pay all kinds of taxes—income taxes, excise taxes, local, state and federal taxes, sales taxes, gas taxes, license fees, assessments. You name it; we pay it.

Tauzin: Wrong.

Businessman: Are you nuts?

Tauzin: Nope. But you're wrong. Businesses do not pay taxes; they collect taxes from consumers. Every business in America is a tax collector for local, state and federal governments. It's the consumers who pay the taxes.

Businessman: Yeah, but we pay them first, and we can't always pass them on to our customers.

Tauzin: Wrong, again.

Businessman: What do you mean?

Tauzin: You are the person who sends those taxes to the government, but you most certainly pass them on to your customers, all of them.

Businessman: No, Billy. That's just not right. Sometimes we can't raise our price to pass on a new tax. Sometimes we have to eat all or part of it. We just earn less profit.

Tauzin: With all due respect, let me disagree. And I'll prove it to you.

Businessman: OK. Go ahead. Try.

Tauzin: Well, let's start here. How do you make a profit?

Businessman: Easy. We try to earn more income than we spend on business expenses.

Tauzin: OK. So your profit is the amount you earn in the business less your total cost of operating the business.

Businessman: Yeah. That's it.

Tauzin: And what makes up your total cost of business?

Businessman: Easy, again. That's the total of all our expenses—salaries, supplies, fuel, raw materials, etc.

Tauzin: Does that et cetera include all the taxes you must send to the government?

Businessman: Well, of course, it does.

Tauzin: Those salaries you pay include payroll deductions, which you send the IRS, right?

Businessman: Right.

Tauzin: And that, too, is part of your cost of business, right?

Businessman: Of course.

Tauzin: So your total costs include all the taxes that you send to the U.S. Treasury.

Businessman: Well...yes.

Tauzin: And if your business is going to survive, you must make a profit, right?

Businessman: Yes, of course.

Tauzin: Well, breaking even doesn't cut it, right?

Businessman: I suppose that's right, too. We could break even or even lose money sometimes. But to stay in business, to keep it going, we've got to eventually make up those losses and turn a profit on top of that.

Tauzin: So, to run a successful business, one that doesn't go bankrupt, you must eventually collect all your cost, all your temporary losses, and collect a profit on top of that.

Businessman: Absolutely.

Tauzin: So here's the proof. You cannot survive as a successful business unless every dollar of cost, including every dollar of taxes you must send to the government—all the income taxes, fees, licenses, assessments, etc.—all the taxes you send to any government must be collected from your customers. Where else would you get the money to pay your business taxes except from your customers. You can't ever begin to earn a profit, of any size, until you've collected all your cost—and that includes all the taxes.

Businessman: I guess that's right. I just didn't think of it that way.

Tauzin: That's the point. Our government doesn't want you to think of it that way. Our government doesn't want you to think of it at all. Because as soon as Americans realize that they, not you, are paying all those taxes, somebody is going to add it all up and get mighty angry.

Businessman: What do you mean "add it all up?"

Tauzin: You see, taxpayers are already pretty upset that "Tax Freedom Day" is now May 9.

Businessman: What's "Tax Freedom Day?"

Tauzin: That's the day of the year that the average American wage earner earns the first dollar he can keep. In other words, up until May 9 of each year every dollar earned goes to some government— local, state or federal. You really pay those taxes over the whole year, but it takes the average person until May 9 to earn enough to pay it all.

Businessman: So nearly half of all our income goes to taxes?

Tauzin: That's the point. But if you add up all the so-called business taxes that are passed on to consumers of everything made in America, can you imagine how big the number gets?

Businessman: Probably more than half a year's income, huh?

Tauzin: You've got it. But, you see, most people don't realize that they're paying their taxes, and they're paying your business taxes, too.

Businessman: But I pay personal income taxes.

Tauzin: Of course you do. And because you are a consumer, you are also paying the business taxes built into the cost of everything you purchase that is made in America. But your own business taxes are passed on to other consumers.

Businessman: So, all of us are double taxed. My business taxes are paid by my customers. But I pay an income tax on my profit and when I spend what's left, I pay somebody else's business taxes as part of the purchase price.

Tauzin: Every time you buy American.

Businessman: What happens when we buy foreign products?

Tauzin: Well, it differs, country to country. But under GATT (the General Agreement on Tariffs and Trade) most major countries who trade with us have a tax system called a value-added tax, a VAT.

Businessman: I've heard of that. How does it work?

Tauzin: A VAT works like this: Every time value is added to a product, that extra value is taxed. And that happens from the raw materials stage to the manufacturing of the final product.

Businessman: So, just like our IRS, every business is taxed and the final products sell for a price that includes all those taxes.

Tauzin: That's right, unless that product is shipped overseas and sold, for example, here in America.

Businessman: What happens in that case?

Tauzin: When a company in a VAT country sells something here, the company files a form with the government over there, and the government sends that company a rebate equal to all of the VAT taxes paid on that product.

Businessman: Wait a minute. Are you telling me that VAT countries sell their products in America tax-free?

41

Tauzin: That's right, at least when it comes to these VAT taxes.

Businessman: So foreign products can come into America and compete unfairly against American products.

Tauzin: It's worse than that. The Kemp Commission on Tax Reform reports that the average small business in America spends $4 complying with the income tax code for every $1 it sends the federal government in taxes. And guess who ends up paying all those costs?

Businessman: Consumers, right?

Tauzin: You got it. So here's the whole story: Consumer products are priced to include all the taxes paid by all the American businesses that produced them, and those prices also include all the outrageous costs of the paperwork, accounting, audits—all the compliance costs of our unbelievably complex IRS code.

Businessman: While foreign products are priced VAT tax-free?

Tauzin: That's right. Is it any wonder, then, why we Americans buy so many foreign-made products and why we have such a big trade deficit. You see, everywhere American products are sold they suffer this unfair IRS disadvantage.

Businessman: That also explains why so many manufacturing jobs have left our country and maybe even why wages in America have been so flat.

Tauzin: Sure. We've got an IRS tax code that taxes Americans twice if they buy American, but only once if they buy foreign. That obviously encourages American retailers to source their products from around the world rather than here in America. And that, in turn, encourages American manufacturing companies to—you guessed it—move their manufacturing to any country outside our own. And there go American jobs and wages.

Businessman: You've got a better idea?

Tauzin: Yes!

Family Of Four Earning $25,000 A Year

Monthly Paycheck Under The Current Income Tax Code

ABC WIDGET CO.
1240 GREENLEAF LANE
ANYTOWN, USA

DATE March 1 , 1998

Pay To
The Order Of ___ Joe Taxpayer ___ $ | **1824** 96 |

Eighteen hundred twenty four and 96/100 ___ DOLLARS

BANK OF PLAINVIEW
Main Branch
P.O. Box 1053
Anytown, USA

John Doe

Monthly Paycheck Under Our National Retail Sales Tax Plan

ABC WIDGET CO.
1240 GREENLEAF LANE
ANYTOWN, USA

DATE March 1 , 1998

Pay To
The Order Of ___ Joe Taxpayer ___ $ | **2160** 00 |

Twenty-one hundred and sixty and 00/100 ___ DOLLARS

BANK OF PLAINVIEW
Main Branch
P.O. Box 1053
Anytown, USA

John Doe

$335.04 INCREASE—18%

43

"THE BEAUTY of the national retail sales tax is its simplicity and fairness," according to Congressman Tauzin. "You decide how much you pay in taxes—and when—by how much you consume. The more you spend, the more you pay in taxes. The less you spend, the less you pay in taxes. In effect, you 'pay to play.' Isn't that fair?" (Photo by Paul Grounds)

"Perhaps the single most urgent policy initiative for the 105th Congress is to replace America's arcane, anachronistic, and anti-growth tax code."

Stephen Moore, CATO Institute

CHAPTER 6

A New National Tea Party

Our country was born in an act of civil disobedience known as the Boston Tea Party. That protest, which we associate with the battle cry "no taxation without representation," was among other things, a tax protest against the British Parliament's imposition of a special tax on tea exported to the American colonies under an equally resented monopoly charter.

As we examine the problem with the income tax code, and the possibility of a better alternative to it, we will again need the power of a grass roots movement to give this proposal life. Nothing short of a national tea party will do. Here's why you should join our effort.

HOW DOUBLE TAXATION WORKS

As my conversation with the American businessman pointed out, only businesses doomed to failure pay income taxes without collecting them from consumers. Soundly-managed, surviving businesses are not so foolish. So businesses, in effect, are tax collectors for the U.S. government.

Here's how it works.

Business operators, beginning with those who work with basic raw materials extraction all the way to those who market products and services at the retail level, carefully calculate the cost of every product and service they sell. They must charge a price that includes all of their costs plus some margin of profit. If any one of them, from farmer, to grain purchaser, to miller, to wholesaler, to distributor to retailer, fails to charge a price that includes all of their costs plus some margin of profit, he will lose money or at best simply break even.

"All of the costs, plus a margin of profit." That's the secret.

Those costs include many things—raw materials, fuel, labor, insurance, etc.

and a thing called taxes, including the cost of the paperwork and filings.

As I have emphasized, the Kemp Commission recently reported that small business in America spends about $4 on tax compliance costs (accounting, paperwork, and filings) for every $1 it send to the U.S. Treasury in income taxes. So the cost of compliance is quite high, estimated to average $900 per person in America, or $3,600 annually for a family of four.

Thus, when one businessman figures the costs of goods or services it must include—and then pass on to the next purchaser—it includes all of the taxes, plus the costs of compliance. When the product or service finally arrives at retail, you and I, the ultimate consumer, pay a final price that includes all of those many business taxes and expenses, plus some margin of profit. We pay all those taxes, all that $4 cost of compliance; we pay all those hidden IRS costs, which economists tell us amount to some 10-to-15 percent of the price of everything we buy that is made in America—our groceries, our utilities, our homes, much of our clothing and even the bottled water we drink.

Unless you buy only foreign-made products, your after-tax dollars are taxed again at this hidden 10-to-15 percent rate. Even then, some American businesses may have imported, distributed and marketed those foreign goods, so the IRS got some additional part of your purchase dollar.

How is the IRS income tax a double-taxation system? Simple. Your income is taxed when you earn it. Then, as a consumer, you pay again another additional 10-to-15 percent in the cost of anything you buy that is made in America.

Suppose you don't spend your money. Suppose you save or invest it. Most interest and investment earnings are, of course, subject to income taxes. But let's assume you don't spend all your assets. You want, instead, to leave them to your children, either during your life or at your death. You'd better proceed carefully because gift and inheritance taxes await you. And, finally, when your children spend any part of their after tax inheritance, they'll pay the hidden 10-to-15 percent IRS tax on those purchases.

Doesn't it just make your blood boil? Why should we have to pay the IRS taxes over and over again on the same money we earn? Shouldn't once be enough?

Under our present oppressive income tax system, the federal government actually sends out a strong signal to us to buy foreign—to use our earnings in support of foreign manufacturers and against every American worker in every manufacturing job. Does that make any sense?

ARE YOU READY YET FOR A TEA PARTY?

As we just described to you, everything made in America carries in its price the full cost of our IRS tax system—that 10-to-15 percent hidden tax. Foreign-made products, for the most part, do not.

Our government has signed trade agreements with our major trading partners that permit them to send their products into America virtually tax-free. It's not that they don't tax their products at home. They do, generally with a value-added tax, which taxes the added value at each stage of the manufacturing process. Those same countries exempt their products from the VAT tax when those products are sent to America for sale.

So foreign-made imported products sit on the retail shelves of America, carrying no VAT tax and no IRS hidden tax, right next to American products carrying the 10-to-15 percent IRS hidden tax. Is it any wonder then that foreign imports do so well in America?

When American products are exported overseas, we do not exempt them from our 10-to-15 percent hidden income tax. So they arrive abroad tax heavy and get taxed again at the VAT rate equal to the domestic product. So, our products sit on the shelf in foreign countries, taxed twice. Yet our nation's competitors are taxed only once. Add it all together and it is easy to understand why we have a $100 billion-plus trade deficit; why America manufacturing jobs are leaving America; why American wages are stagnant, and downsizing is the corporate strategy of the day.

Our government and our income tax code paralyze every American manufacturer, worker, and every wage earner with double taxation. Why do we put up with it?

Well, we don't have to.

WORKERS ARE THE BACKBONE OF U.S. ECONOMY

If you are an income-producing citizen of our country, you ought to be cherished. You provide the energy for our economy. You provide the money to defend our country, to build our infrastructure, to police our streets, to fund our federal courts, and generally to run our federal government. You provide the money to care for our elderly with Social Security and Medicare. You send the dollars that are redistributed to welfare families for subsistence and medical needs. And you share your income with such vital service providers as educators, medical researchers, and criminal enforcement agencies, to mention just a few.

If you are fortunate enough to have the resources to save and invest, you should be doubly cherished. For you provide the money that fuels our financial markets and that creates the capital that provides the rest of us with credit for affordable mortgages to build our homes and our businesses and fuel our credit card purchases. It is you who help finance our government's debt.

And if you are even more fortunate, and eventually accumulate enough assets to pass something substantial on to your children, you should be enshrined in some national citizens' hall of fame. What more could we ask of you than that you give the next generation a leg up on the ladder of success, and, thus, prepare a better future for our country.

Recognizing you as such a valuable citizen, our federal government must certainly have written a tax code that rewards all your hard work, your savings, your intent to leave something to your children.

Wrong. In fact, you couldn't be more wrong.

Our income tax code punishes you when you earn a salary, punishes you when you save, punishes you when you earn on your investments, and punishes you again with gift and inheritance taxes when you give to your children during your life and again when you die. Our IRS code punishes you for doing all the right things. Is there any wonder then that so many people do not?

When our income tax penalizes Americans for earning a living, does it surprise you that so many people find it easier—and even better, in some cases—not to work. My constituents are surprised when I inform them that they need to earn between $8 and $9 an hour to do better than they could, living on welfare—especially those constituents actually earning less than $8 an hour. There are quite a few of them in Louisiana, but it's no coincidence that my state also has an exceptionally high welfare population. Our income tax code certainly encourages them to stay at home and avoid working and paying taxes.

When the tax code penalizes you for earning interest on most savings accounts, is it any wonder that the U.S. has one of the lowest savings rates of disposable income of any of the industrialized nations? If you don't believe me, then just examine the following table.

Big Seven: Personal Savings Rates (a) Percent

	1970	1980	1985	1989	1990	1991	1992	1993	1994
United States	**8.2**	**8.1**	**6.6**	**4.1**	**4.3**	**5.1**	**5.2**	**4.6**	**4.2**
Canada	5.6	13.6	13.3	10.4	9.7	9.6	9.8	9.2	7.6
France (b)	18.7	17.6	14.0	11.7	12.5	13.2	13.7	13.8	13.5
Germany ©	13.8	12.8	11.4	12.4	13.8	12.7	12.9	12.3	11.0
Italy (b)	29.5	23.0	18.9	16.7	18.2	18.2	17.7	15.7	15.0
Japan	17.6	17.9	15.6	14.6	14.1	15.1	15.0	14.7	14.9
United Kingdom (b)	9.2	13.4	10.7	7.2	8.4	10.5	12.8	11.7	10.4

(a) Savings as a share of disposable income (national definitions)
(b) Gross savings
© For 1970—90 western area only, for 1991—1994 unified Germany

In 1994, Americans saved a mere 4.2 percent of their disposable income. You should not be surprised to know that tax codes in those other countries all have generous provisions to encourage savings, while our income tax code does not. Lower savings rates, of course, mean less and, therefore, more expensive money and higher interest rates to finance our homes, business mortgages and daily credit needs.

When our tax laws are written to penalize gifts and inheritance, we are all left with a rather sobering warning from our government: When you've finally beaten the odds and acquired substantial assets, and you are finally old enough to settle down and enjoy them, you had better start giving them away in carefully measured amounts. If you fail, Uncle Sam will be waiting for you at your wake—first in line to take a big chunk of them. In fact, the inheritance tax may be big enough to require your heirs to "sell the farm" to pay taxes. It certainly explains why small business owners and farmers in particular hate America's gift and inheritance tax laws almost as much as they despise the income tax.

Are you warming up to the idea of attending the next American tea party?

Well, there's even more.

IRS IS MOST UN-AMERICAN AGENCY EVER CREATED

No agency of the federal government is more threatening to the idea of personal freedom and liberty than the IRS.

I know that some federal agencies have made themselves pests lately—particularly the regulating agencies with their failure sometimes to use good old common sense, and their failure to respect private property rights. But which agency has the power to randomly audit every American's financial records, without probable cause? Which agency has the power over us to carry on these audits, year after year, until we do little else but live and breathe in fear of the auditor? Which agency presumes your guilt, can threaten you with civil fines and penalties, threatens your future with criminal penalties, and then requires you to prove your innocence—all under a code so complex that 50 different tax advisors will give you 50 different interpretations of your liabilities?

Only with the IRS are we guilty until we prove our innocence. How perverse a notion of freedom. How awful and undemocratic a government policy. How threatening to the concept of personal liberty.

But it's even worse than that.

The IRS tax system empowers Washington with not just the 120,000-plus IRS agents, not just the auditors and bureaucrats who run the system, but most important, the policy makers who write the tax laws and the interest groups who influence them. Talk about raw power. The power to decide how we live our lives; how we make and dispose of income and assets; where we invest; to whom we donate; and even how we raise our families. Tremendous power is in the hands of politicians who can give with one hand and take away with the other; who can create an exemption, a deduction, a credit today and snatch it away tomorrow; politicians who can play us one against the other, rich, poor, middle class, in a class warfare political struggle that only benefits their re-election and further polarizes an all-too-polarized America.

Washington will not easily surrender that much power. Tea parties do not traditionally happen inside government. If citizens want to abolish this awful income and inheritance tax system, which double taxes, penalizes our jobs and wages, encourages us to buy foreign, has disincentives that prevent us from doing all the right things and gives our government power over our lives in ways no self-respecting democracy should ever tolerate, then citizens will have to make it happen, not politicians.

Some of us can only suggest a solution, one learned from our close-up experience with the federal government and from more than a few years of listening and learning. This book presents that solution to you: The national retail sales tax (NRST), a plan to repeal the IRS, personal and corporate income taxes, the gift and inheritance tax laws, and a host of special excise taxes, and replace them with a simple 15 percent national retail sales tax . The NRST includes protections on all income earned below the poverty line so that it is not regressive, treats home ownership better than the current code, lets you decide how much taxes you pay by deciding what portion of your income, above the poverty line, you wish to spend, and ends the disadvantage of our current code on American manufacturing jobs, wages, and products.

Please study the proposal. It's but one of several; however, we think it is superior to all of them. It's not perfect yet. Admittedly, it is a work in progress. We have only begun the process of perfecting it to the extent we can. It is a plan written for all Americans. After you have studied it, then you decide whether to join our crusade for a simpler, fairer system.

If something is worth having, it's worth fighting for in a great American grass roots effort. We'll look forward to meeting you at a tea party somewhere in America.

Yes, we do have a better idea.

"AMERICANS WORK too hard for their money and have too little to show for it,"
said Congressman Tauzin at a recent debate in his home state of Louisiana. "In 1998,
the average American will pay $8,500 in total taxes—that's an inflation-adjusted increase
of nearly 2,000 percent since 1900. What's wrong with this picture?" (Photo by John
Musemeche)

"In my opinion, our challenge will be no less than to pull the current income tax code out by its roots so that it can never grow back."

**House Ways and Means
Chairman Bill Archer**

CHAPTER 7

"Let's Make It Simpler, Fairer, And Flatter"
(A Look At The Competing Tax Reform Plans)

And what is that better idea? First, let's look at the options under serious consideration in Washington.

THE ARMEY FLAT TAX

Steve Forbes' candidacy for the Republican presidential nomination focused a great deal of national attention on House Majority Leader Dick Armey's idea for a flat income tax. The plan is based on a single rate of personal income taxation to replace the multiple or "progressive" tax rate structure and is based on the work of Stanford professors Robert Hall and Alvin Rabushka.

President Reagan's 1986 tax simplification bill went a long way toward a "flatter" tax system. Prior to that, the income tax code contained 14 different rates, ranging from 15 percent on the first taxable income to 50 percent on taxable income above $81,800 for a single person and $162,400 for a married couple. President Reagan's reform plan repealed or modified a host of exemptions and deductions and changed the 14 multiple-rate structure into a two-rate system. But over 4,700 changes since 1986 have created what is practically a five-rate structure. Most flat tax plans would go to a single rate for all personal taxable income.

Income taxes, however, are not limited to personal taxes; they include taxes on personally owned, corporate, and partnership businesses. What didn't get a lot of press attention in the Armey-Forbes plans, for example, is the fact that the 20 percent flat tax on personal income was supplemented by a flat 20 percent tax on business income, which Hall himself described as a VAT tax.

The Armey flat tax starts with a personal exemption of $13,100 and a joint married couple's exemption of $26,000, supplemented with a per child exemption of $5,400. Thus, a family of three would not be taxed on the first $31,400 of income; a family of four, on the first $36,800.

Thereafter, a flat IRS tax rate is applied on the entire balance of the taxable income.

Taxable income, however, is also subject to limitations. For instance, the term does not include income from capital gains or interest earnings on savings, or dividends paid on corporate stock.

Thus, the plan is based on a series of exempted income calculations; thereafter, a flat single rate is assessed on the balance of income, regardless of how that income is spent or otherwise used. The Armey flat tax plan, therefore, contains no specific exemptions or deductions for income that is used to:

> *(1) pay the interest on the home mortgage;*
> *(2) pay the family medical expenses;*
> *(3) provide gifts to churches or charities;*
> *(4) cover non-reimbursed losses;*
> *(5) pay state and local taxes.*

Armey and Forbes argue that the generous personal and family deductions are sufficient to cover such spending deductions (now specifically provided for in the current code).

They correctly argue that to add any of these deductions to their flat tax plan would drive up the flat tax rate.

The rate they have chosen is also of considerable interest. The flat tax plan starts with a 20 percent rate, which is collected for several years and later falls to a 17 percent rate. Congressman Armey readily admits that the 17 percent rate will be insufficient to generate the current income requirements of the balanced federal budget as approved by Congress and that the plan is, therefore, not "revenue-neutral." This means that either:

> *(1) The 17 percent rate must be adjusted upward;*
> *(2) deficit spending and borrowing will result;*
> *(3) Congress could choose to further reduce spending.*

54

The Armey flat tax plan, thus, introduces the controversial policy question of government spending into the tax debate itself.

It has also been suggested that the original 20 percent tax rate would more likely have to be raised to 21 percent or more to be revenue neutral.

A fair comparison of the Armey flat tax plan to any other plan based on revenue neutrality would probably require that a 20-to-21 percent flat income tax rate be used in such a comparison.

The decision to exempt capital gains and interest earnings from "taxable income" has been far less controversial than the decision to exempt dividend income. The dividend income exclusion, Armey and Forbes argue, is based upon the decision to include in their flat tax plans a provision to apply their flat tax rate (20 percent going down to 17 percent) to all business income. They argue that having taxed the business income once, the owners should be able to draw out the profits (through dividends), without a second tax on those dividends.

While technically correct, there is a huge problem with this argument.

First, Steve Forbes was forced to explain in his presidential campaign why a rich individual (who got most of his income through dividends from his corporations) would not have to file or pay a flat tax on those earnings, while every poor working salaried American would be required to file and pay taxes on their incomes. Forbes answer: His taxes had already been withheld and paid by his corporation. While technically correct, this did not quell his critics, nor did it completely answer some nagging questions.

The problem lies with the very nature of income taxation. Taxing income, whether to the worker or to the business, adds a series of new costs to the cost of producing a product or service. Those costs include not only the taxes that are sent to the government, but all of the costs of record-keeping, accounting, audits and filings associated with paying those taxes. All of those costs become part of the sales price of the good or service—all of those costs plus, we hope, a fair enough profit to make the venture worthwhile.

Again, ask yourself this simple question: Where does a business get the money to pay its employees (including the income taxes and other taxes withheld and sent to Uncle Sam), and where does the business get the money to pay its own income taxes (and compliance costs)? Does the business own a money-printing press? Does it have a rich aunt or uncle? Does it have fundraisers at Buddhist Temples? I am being facetious, of course.

55

The point is that the business can find this money to pay its income taxes and its employees' income taxes from only one source—its customers—through the purchaser of goods and services.

Realizing that, ask yourself who eventually pays all of those income taxes. Is it the business owners or is it the business customers?

If your answer is the business customers, then you are beginning to see the problem with the dividend income exemption of the Armey flat tax plan.

The salaried worker, already denied a part of his income through income taxes withheld, finds himself paying for those taxes—and the taxes of his business employer—every time he buys a product or a service from that business. The salaried worker in an income tax world, thus pays taxes twice on the same income. The dividend earner has the problem of now explaining why he should have his dividends tax free while the customers of his business pay his business' taxes. He could argue, again, that his dividend taxes have been withheld and paid by the business and that he, too, like the salaried worker, pays those taxes again when he buys products or services. But the political problem remains. The salaried worker is required to file. The dividend earner is not. Mr. Forbes looks as though he has escaped taxation as he pushes a plan to tax every salaried worker. That's a major political hurdle to overcome.

The 20-to-17 percent flat tax rate on business income was originally described by Professor Robert Hall as a value-added tax. On July 8, 1995, appearing before the House Ways and Means Committee, he admitted: "The Hall-Rabushka flat tax is a value-added tax."

The reason for that admission is quite obvious—it is a value-added tax.

Under this scheme, at every stage of the process of producing American goods and services, a 20 percent (later 17 percent) flat tax rate is applied to the profits of production. From the farmer who grows the grain, to the miller, the transporter, the manufacturer, the distributor, and even the retailer of the box of cereal, all pay the 20 percent flat tax rate on net profits. This tax and its compliance costs add up to a significant part of the cost of the box of cereal.

Because the 20 percent (17 percent) flat tax rate is applied only to American taxpaying businesses, foreign products imported into America will continue to enjoy the same or similar advantage over American products currently subject to the American income tax. Similarly, American exported products, carrying the weight of those income tax costs, go out into the world at a severe disadvantage.

Thus, while the 20 percent (17 percent) Armey flat tax operates as a value-added tax, it is not border adjustable under GATT. The Armey flat tax will continue to discriminate against U.S. labor and U.S. products, and foreign imports will continue to have a huge unfair advantage in the U.S. market.

There are two additional problems with the Armey flat tax plan that deserve very close examination.

While flattening the tax rate, the plan still provides for an income tax. It still requires an IRS with definitions, rates, and regulations to determine what is taxable income. Certainly less complicated than the current code, particularly for individuals, it will still require extensive recordkeeping, accounting, audits, and disputes over the central question of taxable income. For individuals, for example, questions will have to be settled regarding whose taxable income is alimony and which employer-provided benefits are taxable income and which are not. Extensive regulations will be required regarding pension withdrawals. For businesses, the regulations will still overflow with definitions and interpretations of what is and what is not a deductible business expense and what, therefore, is real net profit.

In addition, the Armey flat tax plan does not allow a business to deduct as expenses such things as payroll taxes and interest payments. A business could actually be losing money or just breaking even, with losses or no real profit, and under this plan would be subject to a substantial 20 percent tax on money it didn't earn—money paid out in interest expense or, worse yet—money they have already sent to Uncle Sam in the form of payroll taxes. Talk about unfair, double taxation!

The biggest problem of all, however, is that the Armey flat tax plan still requires an income tax code, and an IRS, no matter how much the current code is reformed.

I have tried to show you in this book how an income tax that started out as a flat one percent tax ended up being today's 5.5-million-word monstrosity. I have tried to describe to you the nature of the beast that is the IRS. Do you believe that keeping an income tax and an IRS is our best option?

The Armey flat tax plan, to its credit, does attempt to protect the growth of both the income tax code and the IRS with a requirement of a supermajority two-thirds vote of each House to raise the rate or to create or expand exemptions. But you and I know that any tax code we agree upon today will come under enormous pressure to change in future years. There we will be pressure to add new rates in return for special exemptions and deductions. We could be right back in the same mess. That has been the story of the income tax, which we, failing to understand, seem always destined to repeat.

More important, continuing to rely upon a non-border-adjustable income tax in the face of more and more free trade—where foreign products made in countries with border-adjustable taxes compete unfairly against U.S. workers and products—seems to me, House Ways and Means Chairman Bill Archer, and many others to be the height of political and economic folly.

Most of those other countries use the value-added tax as their border-adjustable tax, and, therefore, the VAT requires some discussion.

THE VALUE-ADDED TAX

What is the "value-added" concept? How does it work? Has it been tried anywhere else in the world?

The term value-added implies an activity. Something of value has been changed, altered, or improved so that it now has a new and higher value. Value, measured in economic worth, has been added to a product, thus making it worth more.

The value-added tax is designed to define this added value and to assess a tax on it, expressed generally as a percentage of the added value. It may be assessed and collected at each stage of the process, as value is added, measured by the difference in value or worth. Questions of assessment of value must obviously be settled, as well as who is liable for payment, and at what point the tax is collected. What is always clear, however, is that the ultimate consumer, absent an exemption, or rebate, will eventually pay all of the value-added tax assessments as part of the retail purchase price of the products. The value-added tax is used extensively around the world, most notably in Canada and the European Common Market.

The value-added tax, however, has many of the same characteristic effects as the income tax does on U.S. businesses and products. Like the income tax on businesses, the value-added tax is a hidden tax, which accumulates in the cost of a product and remains hidden in the final retail cost. Like the U.S. business tax, the value-added tax increases the price for the consumer and, thus, could have an anticompetitive effect on product sales. And like the U.S. income tax on businesses, if the value-added tax is assessed, in addition to a personal income tax (flat or progressive), it implies double taxation (income taxed once when earned, taxed again when spent).

The fact that the value-added tax is hidden makes it attractive to politicians for obvious reasons. Increasing a hidden tax is an easy way to raise revenue for every government program, worthwhile or not. And even a small increase in the value-added rate generally means huge amounts of new money for the government. Consumers, accustomed to inflation and rising prices, hardly notice. The hidden nature of the tax helps explain its use around the world, and that is the principal reason we reject it.

One of the most attractive features of consumption taxes in general is they get special treatment in international trade agreements, notably GATT. If a value-added tax country wants to allow its businesses to export products tax free, it can do so—generally through a rebate program. Why? Obviously to give those businesses an advantage in the global marketplace.

Here's how it works: A value-added tax country (let's call it "Vatland") creates an export tax rebate for all products made in Vatland and sent to America for sale. Products, thus, arrive in the U.S. with no value-added tax. They sit on the shelf right next to similar American-made products, that carry all of the hidden IRS tax cost in its retail price (which may be 10-to-15 percent of the price). Even considering the cost of shipping and handling across oceans, which product wins? Which product sells the best? Might this tax-free advantage help?

Now, assume an American business sends its products over to Vatland. The cost of the American products contains all the hidden IRS income tax cost (that extra 10-to-15 percent). Under GATT, because this hidden IRS income tax cost is not considered a consumption tax, the U.S. cannot set up a rebate program to make it tax-free. As a result, when the U.S. products arrive in Vatland, that country assesses its value-added tax on the American product, just as our products are taxed, and they sit on the shelf next to one another, this time in a store somewhere in Vatland. Meanwhile, the Vatland product has one tax on it—the value-added tax. The U.S. product has two—the U.S. hidden income tax costs and the Vatland value-added tax. Which product wins? Which sells the best? Remember, even if Vatland has other hidden taxes, even equal to the U.S. 10-to-15 percent hidden IRS costs, it is the U.S. product that now pays both taxes plus the cost of the transoceanic shipping and handling.

Any wonder, then, why we have a huge trade deficit? Why so many U.S. retailers source their products overseas? Why so many U.S. jobs no longer reside here? What can we do?

It's easy. We can replace our income tax on people and businesses with a single consumption tax, that is not a VAT tax on every stage of production. We could then set up a rebate on U.S. exports and assess the consumption tax on imports, ending the intolerable advantage every country with a consumption tax system has over American manufacturing and jobs. That is called border adjustability. We can do this legally under GATT if we have a true consumption tax.

Will the Armey flat tax plan allow us to set up such a border-adjustable tax structure? No. The Armey flat tax is still an income tax, not a consumption tax.

Would the Armey flat tax plan be better for American than the current IRS system? Yes. But the flat tax is still an income tax and still requires an IRS with its obtrusive regulations and enforcement authority.

Is the value-added tax (as part of a flat tax proposal, or even standing alone) the best alternative to the current IRS system? No.

So what is the better alternative? A national retail sales tax.

Our plan is better because it contains no hidden taxes. Our plan is fairer because it taxes us once and only once (and once should be enough). And our plan is automatically border adjustable with no rebate program necessary. It is unquestionably superior to the flat tax proposal, because it alone abolishes the IRS and the income tax.

Do we have a better idea? You bet we do.

THE NATIONAL RETAIL SALES TAX

Supporters of this landmark legislation (HR 2001) predict it will create thousands of new jobs in America, end the exodus of American jobs overseas, and provide a huge economic advantage for American-made products marketed around the wold. Here is a thumbnail sketch of how the bill works (a detailed analysis follows in Chapter 8):

- **INCOME TAX REPEALED:** Personal and corporate income taxes—including income taxes on capital gains and savings—inheritance and gift taxes, and all nontrust fund dedicated excise taxes are repealed.

- **IRS ABOLISHED:** The Internal Revenue Service is de-authorized, as of FY 2001, allowing time to close out previous tax years. No successor agency is established. The Secretary of the Treasury shall administer the new tax system.

● **TAXPAYERS PROTECTED:** Unlike our present system, the burden of proof lies with the government in any dispute with a taxpayer.

● **SALES TAX IMPOSED:** A tax of 15 percent is imposed on the gross receipts from the sale of any taxable good or service in the United States. The amount of tax paid on every transaction must be fully disclosed to the consumer. Under the bill, both states and retail businesses will be able to keep a percentage of the taxes they collect to fully offset administrative costs.

● **REGRESSIVITY:** A tax credit is provided, assuring that all workers will pay no taxes up to the poverty rate. This is accomplished through reduced FICA deductions on every paycheck. (The formula is adjustable for nonworking spouses and children.)

● **EXEMPTIONS:** No tax shall be imposed for any good or service that is purchased for resale; purchased to produce a good or service for retail; exported from the United States; or for the purchase of education or training.

Would a national retail sales tax hurt the poor? Even some critics of the bill say no! Robert Eisner, professor emeritus at Northwestern University and past president of the American Economic Association, wrote in *The Wall Street Journal*:

"The sales tax refunds would leave those at, or close to, the poverty level, and currently without an earned income tax credit cash refund, better off than current law or any of the proposed flat taxes."

The national retail sales tax reverses the relationship between taxpayers and government. Taxpayers—not the IRS—get first crack at their paychecks. Let me say it again: With no federal income tax withheld, workers take home every penny they earn, less FICA deductions. The government only gets its cut when you, as taxpayers, chose to consume. Under this pay-as-you-go tax system, Americans will finally have control over how much they pay in taxes and when.

The beauty of the National Retail Sales Tax is its simplicity and fairness. Those who spend the most will pay the most. Those who spend the least will pay the least. No more income tax forms. No more compliance costs. No more hidden taxes. No more loopholes for corporations and the rich.

Which Plan Is Best For You?

	CURRENT INCOME TAX	FLAT INCOME TAX	NATIONAL SALES TAX
Cost of Filing	Expensive. Costs $600 billion plus per year.	Somewhat reduced.	No cost to individual taxpayers.
Complexity	Very complex. Over 2,000 Internal Revenue Code pages, 12,000 pages of Regulations and 200,000 Court pages.	Withholding continues. Individuals and businesses must still track income and file tax forms.	Individuals do not file. Retail businesses file only sales tax returns.
Hours to Comply	Over 5.4 billion hours per year.	Reduced, depending on the flat tax plan.	Zero hours for individuals.
Penalties	Severe, arbitrary.	Severe, arbitrary.	None for individuals.
Economy	Increases prices, hurts wages, results in decreased savings and investment.	Tax burden still hidden in goods and services. No increase in wages.	Stimulates and rewards savings, investment, and productivity.
Interest Rates	Pushes rates up by reducing savings.	Rates reduced if investment income is not taxed.	Reduced with massive increases in domestic and foreign savings in the U.S.
Investment	Low.	Increased if investment income is not taxed.	Increases investment by U.S. citizens, attracts foreign investment.

Jobs	Hurts U.S. companies and decreases available jobs.	Hurts U.S. companies less.	Makes U.S. manufacturers more competitive overseas. Escalates creation of jobs by attracting foreign investment.
Savings	Decreases savings.	Increases savings.	Dramatically increases savings.
Equality	None. Special rules for special circumstances violate the original Constitution and are unfair.	More. Code still open to adjustment by special interests. Little control.	You have control. All pay the same rate and a fair share. Tax paid depends on life style. Taxes rebated to elderly and poor.
Foreign Companies	Subsidizes their U.S. imports, creating unfair competition to U.S. manufacturers and businesses.	Subsidizes their U.S. imports, creating unfair competition to U.S. manufacturers and businesses.	Foreign companies forced to compete on even terms with U.S. companies for the first time in 80 years.
Government Intrusion	Massive files, dossiers, audits, and collection activities.	Personal files, dossiers, audits and collection activities.	None. No direct tie to individuals, as intended by the founding fathers in the Constitution.

History	Karl Marx included income tax as a key feature in the Communist Manifesto.	Income tax started flat in 1913 then grew out of control with top rate reaching over 90% during WWII. Income tax flattened again to two rates in 1986. Since 1986, there have been 4,700 separate changes to the tax code bringing it again to five income tax rates.	45 states are using a retail sales tax successfully and have proven its efficiency.
Productivity	Decreases.	Increases.	Increases dramatically.
Non-filers	Cash economy which includes criminals and illegal aliens avoid compliance. They do not pay.	Same as current income tax because only the honest person pays income tax.	For the first time, they pay their fair share. Taxes cash in economy.
Visibility	Hidden, layered, complex.	Hidden, layered in prices; withheld from paychecks.	Highly visible, easy to understand.
Congress-ional Action	Used by lobbyists and bureaucrats for social engineering.	The Armey Flat Tax (HR 1040) is now before Congress.	The National Retail Sales Tax Act of 1997 (HR 2001) is now before Congress.

Family Of Four Earning $50,000 A Year

Monthly Paycheck Under The Current Income Tax Code

ABC WIDGET CO.
1240 GREENLEAF LANE
ANYTOWN, USA

DATE March 1 , 1998

Pay To
The Order Of ___ Joe Taxpayer

$ **3436** 92

Thirty-four hundred thirty-six and 92/100 ___ DOLLARS

BANK OF PLAINVIEW
Main Branch
P.O. Box 1053
Anytown, USA

John Doe

Monthly Paycheck Under Our National Retail Sales Tax Plan

ABC WIDGET CO.
1240 GREENLEAF LANE
ANYTOWN, USA

DATE March 1 , 1998

Pay To
The Order Of ___ Joe Taxpayer

$ **4083** 96

Four thousand eighty-three and 96/100 ___ DOLLARS

BANK OF PLAINVIEW
Main Branch
P.O. Box 1053
Anytown, USA

John Doe

$647.04 INCREASE—19%

"MY GOAL is to make April 15 just another day in our lives," Congressman Tauzin explained during a recent debate televised live by Louisiana Public Broadcasting. "Revolutionary change, such as scrapping the federal income tax and abolishing the IRS, will never happen unless Americans demand it." (Photo by John Musemeche)

"Instead of having to pay 15 to 36 percent out of your paycheck each week, you'd pay a flat 15 percent tax at the cash register. A flat tax is good; this is better."

Don Feder, Boston Globe

CHAPTER 8

Why A National Retail Sales Tax Makes Sense For America

Almost any question about a national retail sales tax can be answered by knowing and applying the following principles:

- **No income is taxed until it is consumed.** Capital gains and interest income are not taxed as long as that income is reinvested. The income is taxed only when it is consumed. The same is true for income derived from labor.

- **Deductions are no longer a relevant concept under a sales tax.** Taxpayers, not the government, get first crack at their paychecks. There are no deductions from the paycheck, so there is no need for a tax deduction for state and local taxes or for charitable contributions. All money paid for taxes, or given to charities, is tax free (or equivalent to a 100 percent deduction under the income tax).

- **All goods and services sold at retail are taxed.** The NRST also applies to utility bills, legal fees, video rentals—any and every final good or service that is consumed.

- **No tax should be hidden in prices—all burdens should be visible in the tax rate.** This way we all know what the cost of government is and can make rational decisions about its value relative to other costs we incur. All retailers would be compensated for their paperwork; otherwise, compliance burdens would be hidden in their prices.

- **No business consumption (inputs) is taxed**. Nothing (including paper clips) used to directly or indirectly produce goods for retail consumption is taxed. Otherwise, it would be hidden in the retail price of the final product.

- **The broader the base, the lower the rate—and the rate must be kept as low as possible**. If food, housing and clothing were exempted from the NRST, the rate would automatically double.

- **Businesses do not pay taxes, they only collect them**. Under any tax system—including the income tax—only consumers pay taxes because businesses have no one else to whom they can pass them. More specifically, a business can add the tax and its collection costs into the price of its goods, services, lower wages, or the return on capital to investors or owners. In each case, the cost is borne by individuals as consumers through higher purchase prices, lower wages, or lower return on investment.

- **The government only collects the tax on the value of a good once**. The used-property tax credit gives a 100 percent rebate to the seller for any unused portion of a used good that is sold. This avoids double taxation.

- **Just about any criticism that applies to the NRST also applies to the current income tax system and the flat tax.** The problem of determining whether a good was purchased for business or personal use is the same no matter what type of tax system. In all cases, prices go down and take-home pay goes up—more than offsetting the addition of the NRST.

SHOULDN'T WE BE TAXED JUST ONCE?

The most critical element of the NRST plan is the fact that it does not add a new form of federal taxation; it substitutes one for another. It substitutes a failed income tax system with a simpler, fairer, and more sensible consumption tax system.

Proponents of alternative tax systems almost always dismiss the merits of the NRST with the simple complaint that we'll end up with both a federal income tax and a national sales tax. The truth is quite the opposite. No one, not a single proponent of the NRST, would support the plan unless it first completely repealed the income tax. In fact, we support not only the repeal of the federal income tax, we also support the repeal of the Sixteenth Amendment to the Constitution, which authorizes a federal income tax.

Most important, it is the current income tax code that taxes Americans—first on our income, and then with the hidden 10-to-15 percent IRS cost on everything made in America. And, worse still, it is some of the flat-tax plans that perpetuate double taxation with a flat tax on personal income and with a business or corporation tax, which acts as a value-added tax on American-manufactured products. Only the NRST proposes a single tax collected at a single place, at the point of retail sale. And the NRST starts with a repeal of the federal income tax and the IRS itself. It also contains an important safeguard: Any changes in the rate would require a two-thirds supermajority of both houses of Congress.

HOW DID WE ARRIVE AT 15 PERCENT?

We are often asked the question: How did we arrive at the 15 percent rate? Why not 10 percent? Why not 17 percent or 18 percent? Did we just pick a number out of the sky?

We start with the proposition that in replacing the current income tax system, anticipated revenues should remain constant. Neither should the new system be designed to raise taxes by increasing federal government revenues, nor should the new system produce any less revenue. By keeping the new system "revenue neutral," we avoid any serious challenge that we are proposing a change that will adversely affect any federal government program, leaving the matters of federal government spending and balancing the federal budget to a separate debate on those issues.

HOW DO YOU ESTIMATE ANTICIPATED REVENUES?

There is a constant and never-ending Washington debate on the question of whether revenues should be estimated on a *static* or *dynamic* model. This "Washington speak," in ordinary language, simply means that you can either estimate revenue on the assumption that the economy doesn't change as a result of your proposal, or you can estimate revenues on the assumption that your proposal changes the economy and, thus, produces more or less revenue. One assumption is static (things don't change). The other is dynamic (things will change).

If you remember the old debate during the Reagan years over the Graham-Latta Budget, you will recall a discussion over *"rosy scenario."* Rosy scenario was the name given to the practice of making a budget look better by painting a rosy picture of economic growth. By predicting growth numbers that were particularly rosy, a scenario could be imagined where new revenues would come into the Treasury so that spending cuts could be avoided. This rosy scenario was always based on the theory of dynamic budgeting. The reasoning went something like this:

Our budget makes certain changes in the law (for example, changes in the tax code) which will encourage economic growth. Because of this new growth, people will earn more money, or more people will be employed, and more taxes will be paid into the Treasury. Since all of this new money will be coming into the Treasury, we can balance our budget without doing the tough job of cutting spending. Now aren't we clever?

Such reasoning produced some of the biggest deficits in American history. When the new money based on these rosy scenarios never materialized, or only partially materialized, spending kept right on with borrowed funds, producing larger deficits. Obviously, the abuse of dynamic budgeting produced a very skeptical public and a demand that revenue estimates in the future be based upon static rather than dynamic modeling. Congress responded with the passage of the Budget Enforcement Act of 1990 and the requirement that future changes in the law affecting revenues and spending be based on a concept known as "pay-go."

This is a relatively simple proposal; it requires that an increase in spending must be matched with either a change that produces an equal amount of new revenue or a change that reduces an equal amount of spending somewhere else in the budget. Similarly, any proposed change in the law that decreases revenue must be matched with a change designed to produce an equal amount of new revenue or an equal amount of spending cuts. And all of these changes cannot assume any variations in the economic growth projection—even if it is clear that such changes will almost certainly occur.

With this history as a backdrop, we have approached the process of selecting an appropriate rate for the new national sales tax:

(1) **The NRST should produce the same amount of net revenue in the Treasury as does the current income tax, gift, and inheritance tax laws.**

(2) **The amount of revenue produced by the NRST would be estimated without assuming a change in current economic growth projections—even though there is general agreement that our proposal will produce a growing, dynamic economy.**

(3) **The rate for the NRST would be calculated to fund all anticipated commissions, credits, or rebates necessary to make the proposal revenue neutral.**

(4) **Using the Department of Commerce figures on U.S. consumption, the answer we calculated was 12.9 percent.**

We then asked the following question: What addition to the 12.9 percent rate is necessary to fund the provision that would reimburse the Social Security and Medicare trust funds for the amount necessary to provide an FICA tax reduction equal to the NRST taxes likely to be paid on the first income earned up to the poverty line?

Another simple calculation was required to determine the percentage of the Commerce Department's consumption figures, which added to the 12.9 percent figure, produced a dollar amount equal to the new rate, times the total of all below-poverty income earned in America. The number we arrived at was approximately two percent. Therefore, our final rate to keep the government whole—and to give every income earner a 100 percent credit for all NRST sales taxes paid below poverty income—is 15 percent. (Ironically, this 15 percent rate is nearly equal to the current 10-to-15 percent hidden income tax on the retail price of everything made in America.)

Obviously, the reason to recommend a 15 percent rate rather than a 12.9 percent rate is tied directly to our decision to include two key provisions dealing with the home mortgage deduction and below-poverty income protection. An explanation of these tax provisions and their relative importance to the success of our effort to repeal the federal income tax code and replace it with the NRST is, therefore, necessary.

THE SACRED HOME MORTGAGE DEDUCTION

American tax policy has always favored a central set of tax-favored activities. Simply look at Form 1040 Itemized Deductions, and you will quickly recognize those activities. They principally include: Medical payments, charitable gifts, dependent care expenses, IRA, and other pension plan tax deferrals, taxes paid to state and federal governments, and home mortgage interest deductions.

All of these exemptions and deductions are premised on the notion that income earned and then spent on those protected areas should not be taxed. For someone who chooses not to itemize those expenses, there is a general or standard deduction designed to protect a portion of income—presumably used for those purposes—from the first imposition of the income tax. But each area has a special characteristic worth mentioning.

- The exemption for income taxes already paid to state and local government is obviously designed to avoid a form of double taxation. Because the NRST repeals the income tax, there is no need under our plan for such an exemption.

71

- The exemption for charitable gifts protects gift-giving from taxation. Since the NRST repeals both the income tax and the gift tax, charitable gift-giving is automatically protected in our proposal.

- Tax deferrals for IRA, Keogh, and other pension fund contributions do not necessarily protect that income from all taxation, but operate principally to delay or reduce those taxes. Under the NRST, all savings and investments and their earnings are automatically income tax-free, because, under our plan, all income that is not spent is tax free.

- Medical payments and child or dependent care exemptions are intended simply to encourage taxpayers to care for family members, lest they end up wards of the state. The NRST proposal seeks to address this concern in two ways: first, by eliminating the income taxes on the money used for these (and all other) purposes; and second, by providing the FICA tax reduction to compensate for the NRST taxes paid with income earned up to the poverty line.

- The exemption for the money paid as interest on the home mortgage is clearly intended to encourage homeownership in a society where few can purchase a home for cash. The question we faced as we prepared our proposal was how do you continue to encourage homeownership under a national retail sales tax plan?

THE CURRENT CODE TAXES HOMES TWICE

The current income tax code taxes our home purchases in two ways. First, we pay income tax on the money we earn. With part of what is left, we purchase our residence. In effect, we buy our homes with after-tax dollars. Since the home mortgage interest is deductible, only the payments on the principal (the actual cost of the home) are made with after-tax dollars.

But much of what we pay for when we buy a home has been manufactured in America—the lumber, glue, nails, services, plastics, paint, and many of the furnishings. The price of our home includes this 10-to-15 percent hidden IRS tax effect. We pay taxes on the income we use to buy our home, and then we pay 10-to-15 percent more for it because of the income tax effect on the price of American-made products. We do this over and over again as we sell one home and buy another. This amounts to double taxation on the principal cost of our homes.

THE NRST TAXES HOMES ONLY ONCE

The NRST plan we have submitted encourages and protects homeownership in two ways. By repealing all taxes on income, both personal and business, we eliminate the income taxes on the money we use to purchase our homes, and we eliminate the 10-to-15 percent business income tax effect on the cost of our homes. We then apply the 15 percent national retail sales tax only to the payments made on the principal. The net effect is that we eliminate all taxes on the interest payment portion of the home mortgage and simultaneously eliminate the double taxation of the principal. We simply do not include the cost of financing a purchase (the interest) as a part of the taxable purchase price.

To further encourage homeownership under the NRST, the 15 percent tax is payable in the same monthly installments as the principal so that it is not collected up front in one large sum (unless a home is bought for cash), but rather over the life of the mortgage. Interestingly, in the early years, monthly payments are primarily interest payments, which are not taxed under our plan.

To further insure that the 15 percent national sales tax is collected only once on the principal cost of the home, a used-property credit is allowed against the taxes due on the purchase of a new home whenever you sell one house to buy another.

Thus, the NRST proposal treats the purchase of a home in as good, or better fashion than does the current IRS tax code. It taxes the principal purchase only once, rather than twice; it exempts the home mortgage interest payment, as does the current code; and it collects the new sales tax in monthly installments with a used property tax credit for taxes already paid on the old home when a new home is purchased.

The NRST operates as an encouragement to homeowners, home builders, realtors, and the entire economy, which produces products for the home. The used-property credit further encourages homeowners to move up to bigger and better homes, creating a healthy home market.

Finally, because the NRST does not tax savings and investments, it encourages lower interest costs—a vital component in any vibrant, growing market.

PROTECTING LOW INCOME WORKERS

The current IRS tax code, as we pointed out, provides a general or standard deduction for taxpayers who choose not to itemize their deductions. It also contains personal exemptions and even earned income tax credits for low-income earners. All of these provisions are an attempt to make the current code somewhat "progressive" by protecting low-income earners from the negative effects of increased taxation, placing more of that burden of taxation on middle-and-upper-income earners.

Obviously, there is broad disagreement on how progressive the tax code should be. We regularly hear arguments about taxing the rich and giving to the poor. These class warfare arguments are the natural result of a tax code that confers extraordinary power on politicians, so that they can choose to benefit one set of constituents at the expense of another in the name of whatever philosophical or political motive compels them to do so. It is this power to confer tax benefits and tax burdens that has resulted in over 4,700 changes in the tax code since 1986 alone. Presidents and politicians love that kind of power. Citizens who understand how corrupting and destructive that power can be have come to distrust and dislike it more and more.

Still the question of tax progressivity is a legitimate question that deserves a dispassionate discussion.

When people are asked to consider the relative merits of taxing income or taxing consumption, there is usually a quick and visceral reaction among those who believe that sales taxes are inherently regressive and, therefore, have a negative impact on low-income people. After all, everyone pays the sales tax, and the rate is the same for everyone, rich or poor.

While no honest critic denies the fact that wealthy people tend to spend more than poor people, and, therefore, pay more sales taxes, critics will argue that with sales taxes the poor will always pay a larger percentage of their money than the rich, and, thus, sales taxes are regressive and bad.

CURRENT INCOME TAX IS REGRESSIVE

Are income taxes any better? If all income were taxed at a single flat rate, the answer would clearly be no. Under such a system, the poor would admittedly pay the same percentage of their total income as the rich, but doing so would have a dispropor-tionate and negative effect upon their ability to live on what's left. The poor's ability to pay such a tax would be questioned, and such a system would also be regarded as regressive.

Our income tax code has been endlessly written and rewritten in an attempt to deal with this regressivity/progressivity argument. At different times in the history of the IRS code, so-called progressive rates have been enacted from one percent all the way up to 90 percent on different income brackets. And, from time to time, the amount of first income earned not subject to the taxable rates has been increased to protect the lower-to-middle-income wage earners—all in the name of progressivity.

What has been overshadowed, however, is the effect of business income taxes passed along to consumers. Those taxes and the burdensome cost of tax compliance have produced the 10-to-15 percent hidden tax on everything made in America, and that includes much of the foodstuffs and the essentials purchased by the poor and low-income earners. So as it stands today, the current IRS code actually punishes the poor.

WOULD A NATIONAL SALES TAX BE REGRESSIVE?

It is possible to make sales taxes less regressive, just as the personal income tax has been made, from time to time, less regressive. One of the options often chosen by sales tax authorities is to exempt from the sales tax certain classes of purchases, generally deemed essential. For example, food and drug exemptions and exemptions for housing purchases (food, shelter and health needs) are often singled out. Direct sales tax rebates or exemptions based on age or evidence of poverty or disability are also options. We could have chosen one of these schemes, too.

As we examined these and other options, we concluded that a FICA tax reduction to protect below-poverty income was the best and least complex system to achieve relative progressivity in our national retail sales tax plan. Here's why:

Food and drug exemptions are very difficult to administer. What is justified as food? Are only groceries exempt, or do you exempt fast foods? What about sit-down, high-priced restaurant food? Is champagne included? What constitutes an exempt medicine?

States have struggled with these and many other questions of interpretation and enforcement, and officials across the country have come up with greatly different conclusions.

Similarly, rebates require costly and complex bureaucratic systems, complete with paperwork and all the potentials for fraud and abuse. The same can be said for poverty and disability exemptions. Age exemptions are more easily administered but the potential for problems still exists, and age exemptions standing alone, without means-testing, give equal benefits to rich and poor seniors.

We concluded that a plan to cleanly and efficiently hold most poverty incomes harmless from the effects of our national retail sales tax was available to us without the need for rebates or exemptions. In other words, no gimmicks.

FICA TAXES REDUCED FOR WORKING FAMILIES

Every American wage earner's paycheck is subject to two federal tax withholdings—the IRS income tax withholding and the FICA (Social Security and Medicare) tax withholding. Both significantly reduce a worker's take-home pay. The NRST plan calls for the complete repeal of the income tax and with it the system of IRS income tax withholding. Repeal of income tax withholding will significantly increase every worker's take-home pay.

We do not propose to repeal FICA taxes or the FICA withholding system. Just as we have left spending and budget questions to another debate, we have similarly left Social Security and Medicare reform for another day and another debate. Nothing in our proposal, in any way, affects either the income available to fund Social Security and Medicare or the structure or functioning of either system. But we do reduce the FICA tax withholding on every American's pay check.

Part of our decision to base our NRST proposal on the 15 percent rate (rather than the 12.9 percent) is to produce the revenue needed to reduce FICA taxes.

What we propose is a formula that calculates the approximate amount of the national retail sales taxes paid by a person or family on income earned below the poverty line. It is, after all, that income which is used to purchase the essentials of life—food, medicines, clothing, and shelter. By protecting this income from the NRST, we can effectively increase the progressivity of the tax, so that it affects only income earned (and spent) above the poverty line.

Simply put, we reduce the worker's FICA tax by the amount of sales taxes paid up to the poverty level. (Example: A family of four making $16,000 a year would get an

FICA tax reduction of $2,400.)

The 15 percent rate provides the extra revenue to reimburse the FICA trust fund for the reduced FICA tax rate, thus making the Social Security system and Medicare system 100 percent whole.

Sound complicated? It's not. Here's how it works:

✔ The 15 percent national retail sales tax helps to fund an FICA tax reduction;

✔ Every worker, therefore, gets more take-home pay;

✔ This extra money is enough to pay the national retail sales tax on all purchases made up to the poverty level;

✔ As a result, the NRST is more progressive and less regressive.

Every worker, every income earner, will have the benefit of that protection on the first income earned up to the poverty line. Thereafter, the more you spend, the more you pay in taxes. It is your choice, not that of the IRS. You decide how much in taxes you pay by deciding how much of your income, above the poverty line, you spend and how much you save or invest.

You will only be paying the 15 percent national retail sales tax when you actually spend your money on purchases you choose to make. And when you buy American, you'll be buying goods and services that now cost as much as 10-to-15 percent less, because the IRS hidden tax is also repealed.

Can it happen? Yes. And it should.

There is one category of below-poverty income that remains to be protected in our plan—people that are on non-adjusted fixed income. Let me explain.

For those who do not pay FICA taxes, the reduction of FICA taxes, of course, has no benefits and, therefore, no meaning. For most fixed-income recipients, such as Social Security beneficiaries, retirees, and government pensioners, any rise in the cost of products purchased is offset by a rise in the cost-of-living (COLA) adjustment to their income. But for those on fixed income below the poverty level, without a COLA adjustment, any rise in the cost of living has a direct and negative impact on their purchasing power.

Fortunately, our NRST plan repeals the hidden IRS 10-to-15 percent tax on all American-made products before it imposes the 15 percent national sales tax. For many products, then, there will be a negligible impact on prices. But, admittedly, this will not be true for all American products, and not at all true for foreign-made products. Our NRST will marginally increase the costs of some products. COLA adjustments will be necessary to offset these increases.

WHY WE REPEAL GIFT AND INHERITANCE TAXES

Gift and inheritance taxes should be designed for a single purpose: Guarding against the accumulation of the nation's wealth in the hands of the few to the exclusion of the many. Put another way, gift and inheritance taxes should be designed to insure that America always has a strong, vibrant middle class.

But gift and inheritance taxes have become both cruel and destructive. Gift and inheritance taxes have become, over time, not a protection of the middle class, but the archenemy of small businesses, family entrepreneurs, and family farms, which make up the core of the American middle class. Gift and inheritance taxes have become a major hindrance to the transfer of middle-class family assets from parents to children.

When a tax structure forces the sale of a family farm, or a family business, so that the inheriting children can pay taxes, middle-class values are destroyed rather than protected; family businesses are lost rather than created.

Gift and inheritance taxes now aimed at middle-class families rather than the wealthiest among us send the worst type of message. Rather than a message encouraging Americans to save for their senior years and save enough to pass something valuable on to their children—to give them a head start on their own middle-class independence—gift and inheritance taxes do just the opposite.

When this negative message is combined with the punitive effects of our current income tax code, this is what we hear: If you earn income, we'll tax your earnings; if you save money, we'll tax your savings; if you invest your earnings, we'll tax your gains; and if you dare to try and leave what's left to your children before you die, or in the event of your death, we'll punish you for earning, saving, investing, and for giving your assets to your children. What's more, with the hidden 10-to-15 percent income tax on American-made products, we punish you for spending your money on anything but foreign-made products. What an awful message. Could our nation's tax laws be more cruel or inappropriate?

Under HR 2001, we propose a complete repeal of all federal gift and inheritance taxes, as well as repeal of the federal income tax. The income tax on salaries, earnings, profits on capital gains, income earned by individuals, partnerships, associations and corporations—until and unless that income is spent for final consumption at retail level—is gone. As such, our proposal, admittedly, permits the savings and investment of unlimited sums at a zero percent tax rate. This potential for the few to accumulate the wealth of our nation will surely be a seriously-debated feature of the plan. But where do you draw the line if you wish to keep any part of the gift and inheritance tax laws? What's the point of accumulating income if you never enjoy it by spending it? Experience tells us that heirs know what to do with their inheritance; they enjoy it by spending it. And when they do, the NRST taxes that spending.

We also believe that excise taxes on specific products will create a new double taxation when the NRST is enacted. Therefore, we include in our proposal, the repeal of all excise taxes not specifically dedicated to a trust fund. Here is a list of those repealed and those retained:

- **ELIMINATED** — cars, boats, aircraft, jewelry, fur, gas-guzzler tax, tires, vaccines, sporting goods, alcohol, and tobacco.

- **RETAINED** — diesel fuel, special motor fuels, gasoline, aviation fuel, coal, and commercial waterway transportation fuels.

HR 2001 MEANS MORE MONEY AND MORE FREEDOM

Under our plan, income taxes on individuals and businesses (including capital gains) would be repealed, along with the income tax withholding and quarterly and yearly filings. The IRS would be disbanded and some of its personnel shifted to the Treasury. Wage earners would take home all of their income, less FICA (Social Security and Medicare) taxes.

But those FICA taxes would be reduced to compensate all wage earners for sales taxes paid with income up to the poverty level. (Money collected on sales taxes on that income would flow back to the Social Security and Medicare trust funds, making the trust funds whole.)

A 15 percent national sales tax would be collected at the point of retail sale for consumption on all goods and services purchased in the U.S. or purchased overseas for consumption in the U.S. The national retail sales tax would not apply to:

(1) Purchases at wholesale for resale;
(2) purchases for use in making a product for sale;
(3) educational expenses;
(4) home mortgage interest expenses.

The NRST would be collected by America's retailers (who would be paid a commission of one-half of one percent of the taxes collected) and by the state sales tax authorities (which would also receive a commission of one percent of the taxes collected). For the four states that have no sales tax, a federal collection system would be deployed if they opted not to create one or contract with another near state to collect. National retailers would have the option of sending sales taxes directly to the Treasury.

The national retail sales tax would have to be expressed as a separate item on the price of the product or service, as opposed to "hidden" in the cost of the product. Americans will, from then on, see the true cost of their government.

Neither the rate of the national retail sales tax, nor any of its exemptions, could be altered, raised, or lowered, without a supermajority two-thirds vote of both houses of Congress.

CROOKS WOULD PAY SALES TAX, TOO

The NRST would also tax purchases with money now earned in both the legal and illegal underground economy. These freeloaders, who already get away with paying no income taxes or FICA taxes, would get no special breaks from the repeal of the income tax code or from reduced FICA taxes. But every time the dope dealer, illegal immigrant, or other income-tax evader used any of that underground income to make a legitimate retail purchase, the rest of us would benefit from the collection of a 15 percent national retail sales tax on goods and services.

The NRST would also make honest citizens out of those of us who make an occasional sale or participate in a garage sale. Typical occasional and garage sales are not subject to the 15 percent tax, and, of course, since all income taxes are repealed, there is no tax avoidance on the income earned.

Admittedly, fraud is a problem in every tax system. Our plan would be no exception. But because the states have a huge incentive—their retained commission—they would be more likely to enforce collections for the NRST just as they would for their own sales taxes. Additionally, retailers who honestly collect the NRST on their sales have a big incentive to prevent unfair competition from anyone who might try to avoid collecting the tax. And, finally, the plan provides a reward to those who help report and uncover such fraud.

So it boils down to this: If you operate in the underground economy, you won't like this plan. But if you work hard and are tired of double taxation to pay for these freeloaders, you'll love it. If you think we ought to punish people for buying American and reward those who buy foreign, you'll hate this plan. But if you're sick and tired of seeing manufacturing jobs fleeing the country—and you'd like to see more Americans working and fewer on welfare—you'll clap for joy when the NRST is adopted.

If you've had enough of a tax code that costs the American people more than $300 billion in compliance costs a year to collect $650 billion in taxes, then get aboard this train. If you've had enough of paying double taxes, then join this revolution. If you think it's time for us to stop punishing people for earning income, for saving, for investing, for leaving something to their kids, and for buying American, then be silent no more.

And if you are mad as hell and determined not to take it anymore from an IRS that is the most invasive and undemocratic agency we've ever created, an agency where you're guilty until you're proven innocent, and where every IRS office can have its own interpretations of rules and regulations that few can understand, then join us in the fight to repeal it all.

Finally, if you love liberty, then join the new Sons and Daughters of Liberty at a tea party somewhere near you and be a foot soldier in the national effort to wrest power away from Washington, D.C., and return it to our people.

With the NRST, you decide—not the government—how much in taxes you'll pay, by deciding how much of your above-poverty income you spend. And you make all the choices with your own hard-earned money.

Freedom of choice: Isn't that what America's all about?

IN TRYING to drum up support for sweeping tax reform, Congressman Tauzin has appeared on radio and television nationwide, hoping to hammer home his message. "What if I told you that we could create thousands of new jobs in America," Tauzin recently said to a radio audience, "end the exodus of American jobs overseas, and provide a huge economic advantage for American-made products around the world. Would you be for it? Of course, you would!" (Photo by Frank Bordonaro)

"Replacing the federal income tax is the right thing to do and this is the right time to do it."

Senator Richard Lugar

CHAPTER 9

Sons And Daughters Of Liberty, Unite

How does an honest-to-God grass roots movement happen in America?

In today's political jargon, a campaign, a story, or an issue that shows any signs of life is said to have *legs*. Without *legs* a campaign stalls and soon falters. Without *legs* a story gets old, people lose interest, and soon nobody bothers to repeat it. Without *legs* an issue no longer excites us, and it soon dies from inertia—becoming yesterday's cause celebre, as exciting as day-old fish.

Legs. Now that's a good metaphor. Picture the constantly moving legs of a millipede as it scrambles along a leaf. Or picture an army on the march as its thousands of legs swing along in unison. Or picture the thousands of Egyptian legs straining to move huge sandstone blocks along together to form the massive pyramids at which we still marvel thousands of years later.

Good old legs carry us about from place to place in our daily lives without our being particularly conscious of their importance.

Political pundits use the term *legs* to define that quality in a story or campaign that keeps us coming back for more. More simply than an energy or a sign of life, *legs* determine whether this thing is going somewhere; that it not only has momentum, but there is fuel in the furnace and wood in the stove; that people are moving from awareness, to interest, to adherence and advocacy.

Legs implies that an issue has a resonance that won't go away, like the melody you hear in the morning that stays with you all day. *Legs* implies that the issue has an attractiveness which compels people to first pay attention, then to focus their awareness and interest in the subject, as the campaign or story unfolds or the issue is debated.

The idea of replacing the income tax with a fairer, flatter, and simpler tax system has political legs. But it needs plenty of the human kind, too, the physical legs that you and I can use to carry this issue across the heartland of America and into Washington, D.C.

Becoming a member of the movement to repeal the income tax is not difficult. There are several groups already organized and eager for new believers, such as Citizens for an Alternative Tax System and Citizens for a Sound Economy (See Appendix C).

Joining an existing organized group is not, of course, your only option. Forming a local, state, or even national group of your own is not only possible but perhaps a more interesting and challenging option. Successful grass roots movements benefit from the sheer number of its units, particularly if coordination and other forms of cooperation among those units is achieved.

There is also more than ample room for individual efforts, combining time-proven forms of communication, such as town meetings, petitions, postcard and letter-writing campaigns, letters-to-the-editor, etc., with new forms like e-mail, fax, and video conferencing. A single person or couple, working from an Internet work station at home, can create a power center of news, information, and grass roots lobbying on behalf of the repeal effort.

Let me be quite candid with you. I have no idea whether we can, collectively, create the kind of American grass roots movement that I know will be required to "rip the income tax out by its roots" and replace it with a better system for our country.

I know of a thousand good reasons why we should fail; a thousand barriers we will encounter; and a thousand credible people who will argue persuasively that such a radical change is too risky and that the status quo is much safer. After all, we can simply keep amending the code. I know many less-credible, less-qualified people, who without much thought, or even without the truth, will dismiss this effort and persuade others to do so. And I know still others who will outright lie about these and similar proposals because it serves their interests to do so. It is so much easier to confuse and destroy an idea than it is to honestly consider, analyze, and debate it.

Yes, I know a thousand good reasons why this all may be futile, why all our best efforts may be in vain.

But I know of one good reason why we must try: Because it is the right thing to do for our country. I know it is. And now, you know it, too.

HOW TO "WORK" CONGRESS

Look at the faces of the members of Congress and you are looking at the face of America. Talk to them, one on one, and you are speaking with the very same people you could be speaking with on nearly any street, in almost any community, in almost any corner of their districts. Generally speaking, each member looks like and has a personality not very different from the average American you will find in his or her home district. Here are some interesting little known facts about the U.S. Congress.

Believe it or not, most of the members are not lawyers. Actually only about 29 percent hold law degrees, and of those, none are permitted to practice law while they serve in the Congress. Of the over 70 percent who are not lawyers, you will find truckers, farmers, ranchers, doctors, dentists, professors, homemakers, laborers, corporate executives, small businessmen and women; in short, a fair sample of working America.

Most members do not make a career of Congress. Actually the average tenure during the 1970's was 8.7 years. In the 1980's, the average tenure dropped to 8.3 years, and in the 1990's, it dropped to less than eight years. A large number of members came to Congress with some experience in government on the local or state level, but an increasing number do not. And, more and more, members come with their own self-imposed term limit, often a promise made during a successful election campaign.

Most members do not live in and become part of the beltway, a term given to those whose lives are centered within the Interstate 495 beltway that encircles the greater Washington, D.C., area. Many members choose to keep their families in their home district and regularly commute to Washington. Others, while maintaining one home in the Washington, D.C., area, continue to maintain their primary residence in their hometown within their state and district, making frequent trips between the two, spending whatever time they can with local constituents, family, and friends.

So here you are, convinced that the IRS and the income tax must go, and knowing that your U.S. Congressman and your two U.S. Senators, along with a majority of others like them, are the people who can make it all happen. How do you get to them? How do you help convince them? What can little ol' you do in this big equation to make them take this debate seriously and join the cause?

Here Are My Top Ten Suggestions:

1. **You cannot be expected to do it alone.** None of us can. Only through networking with like-minded people do we have any hope of success. Join a support organization. Or, if you prefer, start one of your own or affiliate with another.

2. **Learn the issue well.** Ignorance and outright demagoguery will be our greatest opponents, and they will have the upper hand at first. It is always easier to trash a proposal than to defend it. If you are to be credible in the national effort to repeal the income tax and the IRS, you have to know why it's important to our country to do so, and you must know everything you can know about the rational alternatives— including our proposal for a national retail sales tax.

3. **You cannot be silent and expect someone to speak for you.** Members of Congress listen more than you think they do. They listen to all kinds of voices—to the voices of organized interests, yes, but also to the voices of people they trust. Often those people are staffers, even other members whom they have come to admire and trust. Most often those people are the folks who trusted them in the first place—their friends, neighbors and constituents back home. You should be one of these people. You should know who your congressman and senators are. You should be one of the voices they hear regularly.

4. **Personal letters or messages are respected**. I have a computer system in my office that will respond to any computer or organized mailing received on a given issue. But, I pay much more attention to personal mail. Every member of Congress knows the difference between mail that is generated and mail that is personal from trusted constituents. Organized mailings are noted properly and can have an effect on a member's thinking. But personal mail, e-mail, faxes, and telephone calls are entitled to a greater degree of respect—and they receive it. Personally communicate your messages.

5. **Your voice has great significance if it is recognized.** The ideal situation is one in which you are one of those credible and trusted constituents whose personal message is warmly and respectfully

reviewed because the congressman or senator knows you and recognizes your voice. Develop a personal relationship if possible.

6. **Town hall meetings are great places to gain a recognizable voice.** Members of Congress and senators spend large sums of campaign dollars trying to get you to know them. They spend equally large amounts with pollsters and consultants, all in an effort to get to know you—how you think, what you think, if you vote, and how you vote. You do them a favor when you provide this information. How? By attending a town hall meeting, identifying yourself, and letting them know how you think and what you think about things important to them—like what to do about taxes. Soon they'll recognize your face or your voice. It works.

7. **Work to educate the staff.** A Congressman or senator will turn to his or her staff first for an understanding of an issue. The old adage is: Educate the staff, and you educate the member. You can find out who they are by contacting any one of the official offices (at home or in D.C.) for a list. You should look for: (1) The AA (administrative assistant) or chief of staff—that is the person who runs all of the congressman or senator's offices, often the principal confidant and advisor; (2) the L.D. (Legislative Director)—this is the person who directs the work of the legislative or issue-oriented staff, as opposed to constituent service; and (3) the L.A. (legislative assistant) in charge of tax issues—the person assigned the job of handling the legislation and votes on tax related measures. Among these staff members, you will find the person most likely to help shape the member's understanding of our issue. Once you know who that person is, aim your education efforts there.

8. **Speak out publicly**. Use radio talk shows, letters-to-the-editor, and other public forum opportunities to be heard on the issue. I promise you, politicians react to public sentiment.

9. **Use personal stories when appropriate**. Members of Congress love to tell good stories. They like to hear them, too. If you have a good personal story that helps to make your case, bring it out early and use it.

10. **Be Persistent**. Never stop. Never give up. Things do not easily change in Washington, D.C., and we're talking about revolutionary change. Repealing the IRS and the income tax will take one of the hardest-fought political battles in our nation's great history. But it is worth the effort. If your congressman or senator isn't a convert yet, keep preaching. If they don't like one of your arguments, use another. We have plenty. Keep trying.

Every Consumer Purchase Is Taxed TWICE Today

ONCE: when income tax is withheld from consumer's paycheck
AGAIN: when consumer pays hidden business taxes

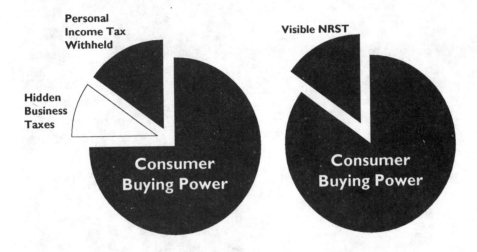

Once is Enough!

"THE IRS POWERS to investigate and examine taxpayers are oppressive," Congressman Tauzin explained during a debate in Oklahoma City. "Virtually all of your constitutional rights regarding search and seizure and due process do not apply to the IRS. So here's the fix we're in: The income tax code is a mess, and the IRS is out of control. It's time to scrap them both and start with a clean sheet of paper." (Photo by Paul Grounds)

"We should repeal the Internal Revenue Code and start over."

Former IRS Commissioner
Shirley Peterson

CHAPTER 10

21ˢᵗ Century America: A Vision

Let's imagine that HR 2001 has finally become law. We have just completed the transition. The American income tax is gone—buried for good. The IRS is disbanded with some of its agents and employees transferred to other departments of the Treasury, others entering other government service, and still others seeking work in the private sector.

Most Americans have received their first paycheck under this exciting new system. The envelope is open, and a broad smile slowly replaces the shock of first discovery. It is truly hard to believe the bottom line, so dramatic is the increase in take-home pay. Where did it come from, some wonder, betraying one of the most diabolical aspects of the old income tax withholding system. Many wage earners never thought of the income tax withheld as a part of their salary—their own money—taken by the government before it so much as reached their hands.

But here it is now—in their hands at last—their own money. Americans can do with it as they choose. Money they never saw before, except at tax-refund time, and then only after the government had used that money for a year interest-free. Their paychecks now represent, for the first time since 1913, all of the wages of their hourly, daily, and weekly labors with only Social Security and Medicare taxes deducted. And even those deductions are smaller than before (representing reduced FICA taxes under our plan).

Every American worker has been given a big salary increase. This additional money, formerly income taxes withheld, is really their money; theirs to spend; theirs to save; theirs to donate; theirs to invest anytime, anyway as they—not the government— see fit.

For some, the salary increase is a welcomed chance to pay down accumulated debt. For others, the pay boost will buy a needed item that had been put off because of a lack of funds or credit. For all, the bigger paycheck is welcomed relief following years of wage stagnation and ever-increasing tax and price increases. For wage earners, the new paycheck represents new personal freedom, opening up options that their old, smaller paychecks never allowed. Yes, there is a good reason to smile.

AMERICAN ECONOMY TAKES OFF

Suddenly, there is something strange going on in the marketplace. Businesses all over America are re-examining their budgets and their business plans for the next quarter. Owners, partners, and corporate boards are poring over an extraordinary set of numbers, each trying to develop aggressive new strategies.

Some of the suppliers have already discovered that the cost of doing business in American has gone down dramatically. The company that sells the raw materials has dropped its prices because a competitor has undercut their old price list. Neither will pay any income taxes on their business this year, and neither has had to prepare or file the old IRS tax forms. They are aggressively going after each other's customers, and they are now able to pass on some of those anticipated tax and compliance cost savings. They are also identifying new customers who formerly sourced their products from offshore suppliers.

As U.S. companies in the chain of manufacturing begin to benefit from these new competitive prices, they, too, find their competitors undercutting old price lists. In freely competitive areas, prices fall rapidly. Businesses that try to keep these new savings to enhance their profits, watch in dismay as their market shares drop.

Meanwhile, retailers in America, operating on a slim one-to-two percent profit margin because of the fiercely competitive nature of their businesses, pass most, if not all, of their tax savings on to their customers. It's the nature of the free-market system. It's the American way at work.

CONSUMERS OPTIMISTIC, TOO!

Consumers are walking into these retail outlets armed with more money—a big boost in their weekly paychecks representing all of the formerly withheld income taxes and reduced FICA taxes. With this new buying power, they confront a visible 15 percent national sales tax (partly offset by reduced retail prices), and they do what comes naturally—they purchase. They see the national sales tax—and they feel its impact upon their purchases—but they purchase, nevertheless, knowing they now buy products with dollars that have not already been taxed, and knowing this is the only place they are taxed at the federal level. They also know that everybody around them is paying the same tax—no loopholes for the rich, no exemptions for those favored by politicians.

92

Everyone is contributing, according to the size of their purchases, to the necessary cost of the federal government.

And they are doing something even more remarkable: They are, more and more often, choosing American-made products. Why? Because today, with the repeal of income taxes, American-made products can be as much as 10-to-15 percent less expensive. And since the national sales tax of 15 percent is applied equally to imported foreign-made products, American products are much more competitive.

So as American businesses are looking at these new numbers—lower product costs and greater consumer demand—they begin to revise their business plans. *FOR RETAILERS*: "Let's stock more of those American-made products, and let's keep our price below the store across the street." *FOR WHOLESALERS*: "Let's source more of those American-made products, and let's keep our prices below those import wholesalers." *FOR U.S. MANUFACTURERS*: "Let's build more of our products here in the U.S. where there's no income tax, and let's think about relocating those plants we built overseas." *FOR INVESTORS*: "Let's invest in that plan to build a U.S. manufacturing plant."

And, finally, *FOR ALL AMERICAN BUSINESSMEN*: "Let's consider hiring more people to make, market and sell those U.S. products that are now so much more competitive, not only here but overseas, too. Let's think about increasing our export business now that our U.S. products can be produced less expensively."

The U.S. marketplace is humming with excitement.

Now, because investment income is no longer subject to our income tax—no longer penalized—investment capital is suddenly more available at more affordable interest rates. Now, because interest on savings accounts is no longer taxable as ordinary income, savings rates expand, and more capital for investment is available. Now, because of these capital accumulations and expanded savings rates, interest rates fall and mortgages become even more affordable.

An investment and building boom results, and the U.S. labor and manufacturing base responds with increased activities. More wage earners, with more buying power and more incentive to save and invest their earnings in the U.S. economy, are like a sleeping giant.

The new expanding economy means more opportunities for American workers and investors—less dependency and less poverty. Government income, once hard pressed to provide adequate health care, retirement, and social service funds for the many people who depend heavily upon government programs, are beginning to rebound, replenished with the same infusion of capital from which the general economy has benefited. Those systems, Medicare, Medicaid, Social Security, welfare, public housing, etc., are now less stressed and more adequately funded. As more opportunities are created in the workplace of America, "workfare over welfare" becomes an achievable goal. More workers and fewer government dependents on the system begin to restore the ratio of workers to retirees, further stabilizing retirement systems.

But there is a shift in thinking even more positive and exciting than the good economic news. **Americans feel good again about America!**

There is a growing realization that we no longer have to fill out income tax forms; that we don't have to keep track of everything we earn and spend in the hope that some of it will eventually be exempt or deductible; that we don't have to waste so much of our time trying to outsmart the IRS, worried that we might be caught on some error and declared guilty unless we can prove our innocence.

At long last, government is less a part of our daily living. We are suddenly and significantly more in charge. Power has shifted, like some great tectonic plate moving an entire continent. That's right. Power has shifted from Washington, D.C., back to the people. A slumbering giant has awakened.

FINALLY, IT'S NOW UP TO US!

We now decide what we do with the money we earn, and we decide how much of it we pay in taxes by deciding how much we spend on taxable consumption and how much we save, invest, or donate.

We are presumed innocent again. Our government no longer requires us to prove it. We are suddenly a freer people. Our liberty is more secure. We are masters of our own fate. We are, most importantly, a nation of, by, and for the people once again.

It is this new vision of America, more than anything else, that compels all of us in the tax-reform movement to repeal the IRS and the income tax, and to give America a simpler, fairer tax code. Isn't it time for the world's freest people to have the world's fairest tax system? If you share that vision, please join us. America can not afford to fail.

Are you ready for another Tea Party? Together, we can make April 15 just another day.

NEARLY 15,000 PEOPLE attended the "Scrap the Code" debate in Bakersfield, California. President George Bush and former First Lady Barbara Bush were among those in attendance. Prior to the debate, Congressman Tauzin explained his tax reform plan to Mr. and Mrs. Bush. Pictured at far left is Congressman Tauzin's communications director, Ken Johnson, who helped to organize the nationwide tax tour. (Photo by Congressman Bill Thomas of California)

"Billy's absolutely right. This isn't just about money. This is also about freedom in America."

House Majority Leader Dick Armey

APPENDIX A

Frequently Asked Questions About HR 2001

Q: Assuming the national retail sales tax plan is adopted and the income tax repealed, can't Congress reinstitute an income tax and then we'll have both?

A: Yes, unless we all get behind and pass HR 2001 and the repeal of the Sixteenth Amendment to the Constitution (which authorized the income tax). If we can successfully repeal the Sixteenth Amendment, an income tax can be rendered unconstitutional by the language of the new amendment.

Q: What about the FICA taxes? Couldn't a future Congress simply raise the FICA rates once the income tax is repealed?

A: Yes, but Congress can do so now. The real protection against Congress doing such a "bait and switch" is to prohibit the FICA receipts being used for any purpose other than those intended (Medicare and Social Security) and the passage of a Balanced Budget requirement so that FICA trust funds are never borrowed by the Treasury (as they are today).

Q: Isn't a national sales tax a regressive form of taxation, hitting the poor hardest since they must spend most of their income to live?

A: Yes, it would be—if the plan did not have some way of exempting low-income producers. Ours does. Our plan completely insulates all wages earned below the poverty line from the payment of the national sales tax by reimbursing the wage earner through the FICA tax withholding for national sales tax collected on all income earned up to the poverty line for that family.

But there is a double bonus for low income earners under our plan. Since we repeal their income taxes, they have more disposable income to spend. And since we repeal the hidden IRS cost (10-to-15 percent) on all products made

97

in America, products should be less expensive. More money to spend on less expensive products is a good deal by anybody's reckoning.

Q: What about middle-class wage earners? If your plan helps the poor, doesn't that mean that the middle class takes it on the chin again?

A: Wrong. This time we got it right. Middle-income wage earners get the same FICA tax credit that low-income earners get on that portion of this income up to the poverty line for that family. All wage earners are treated the same. And all wage earners get the double bonus of more income to spend (no income taxes and reduced FICA taxes) and less expensive American-made products to buy. All wage earners will also benefit from a growing economy inspired by the new fair treatment for American-made goods (more jobs and better wages). There will be new incentives to save and invest (no more income taxes on income from wages, savings, or investments).

Q: Will wage earners have to pay the national sales tax all year and then get their FICA tax credit at the end of the year?

A: Only our mean-spirited income tax code treats you that way. The IRS keeps your withholdings all year until you file for and prove your right to a refund.

Our plans gives you the FICA credit automatically on each of your paychecks, by simply reducing the FICA tax withheld. That's fair treatment.

Q: What about state sales taxes? Will the national retail sales tax be collected in addition to our state sales tax?

A: Yes. Our plan repeals the federal income taxes and federal gift and inheritance taxes and replaces them with the national sales tax. States would keep their authority to levy whatever state sales taxes they wished.

Q: My state has an eight-cent sales tax. With the national 15 percent tax, are you saying we'll have to pay a total 23 cents sales tax?

A: Yes. But you're paying just about that much now—plus you're paying income taxes.

Remember, the income tax cost on everything made in America adds a hidden income tax of 10-to-15 percent which you're paying now on top of your state sales tax. That's a total of 18-to-23 cents, plus you're paying income taxes on those dollars before you spend them. That's double taxation. Our plan says once is enough

Q: But if we see the 23-cent tax on our purchase, won't that discourage us from buying things? And won't that hurt retail sales?

A: No. Think about having a big salary increase. Your check just got bigger because the federal government no longer withholds any income taxes and your FICA taxes are reduced. You now have more of your own money to spend or save or invest. Go look at you last check stub. Look at the amount the government withheld in income taxes. Now imagine you get to keep that amount each payday.

Remember, too, that everything you buy made in America just got 10-to-15 percent less expensive to make. Some, if not all, of that savings gets passed on to you the consumer.

Now, you've got more money to spend for less expensive American-made products. You get to decide. Will you buy less because of the sales tax? We think not.

And, finally, bigger ticket items are usually purchased on time and on credit. The sales tax is paid the same way, factored over time.

Q: You keep referring to the hidden income tax cost on American-made products. Is there a comparable tax cost on foreign-made imported products?

A: There could be and likely is. But the big tax on foreign-made imported products is generally the VAT imposed on products in their home country. Here's the problem:

When the foreign-made import comes to America, the foreign home country generally rebates the tax to the company that made the product. The foreign government even rebates the VAT to Americans who go over there to buy a product that they bring back to America.

What this means is that the foreign-made import comes to America without the VAT cost in it.

So our American products carry a hidden income tax cost of 10-to-15 percent, and the foreign-made product carries no VAT. Guess who all too often was the competitor for our dollars. Guess why so many jobs are leaving America.

The same thing happens when we send our products over there. Our American-made products arrive with the full income tax cost on their backs and then get promptly taxed with the local VAT tax (which, of course, is carried by the local products, too). So our American-made products carry two tax loads.

Is it any wonder we have a $100 billion-plus trade deficit?

Our plan changes all that. Here in America, both American-made products and foreign imports would pay the same 15 percent national retail sales tax. Our local products would no longer suffer a 10-to-15 percent disadvantage. With a new advantage, that big, can you imagine how much more often American-made products will win our purchase dollars? Can you picture the boost to American manufacturing, jobs, and wages?

Abroad, the same thing happens: Under the NRST, our products no longer carry the hidden income tax cost, they carry only the same VAT placed on local products. Again, American exports no longer suffer a 10-to-15 percent disadvantage. Result: Advantage for American exports, jobs, and wages; 19,000 new jobs for every $1 billion in exports.

Q. How is insurance treated under the NRST?

A: Insurance can be a service, an investment, and a reimbursement all at once. Its treatment in a sales tax world is admittedly a little tricky.

A sales tax system must either: 1) Tax the full amount of the premium and exempt purchases made with insurance claims; or 2) tax purchases made with insurance claims with the tax also being reimbursed by the insurance company. HR 2001 generally follows the second option, to avoid the administrative problems associated with the exempting insurance-reimbursement purchases. Here are three examples:

- **Life Insurance:** Life insurance premiums have two parts, an investment component and a service component. The investment portion is not consumption and would not be taxed (when a life insurance claim is paid, it will be taxed when those dollars are consumed). The service component, which represents the overhead of the insurance company necessary to provide the insurance service—a relatively small portion of the premium—would be taxed.

- **Casualty Insurance:** An auto or homeowner's policy premium would: 1) have to cover the costs of the NRST on the repair of parts and services of a damaged car or the replacement of stolen jewelry, for instance; and 2) be taxable on the portion of the premium that represents the intermediate service.

- **Health Insurance:** Likewise, the health insurance premiums would have to cover the reimbursement for the taxes paid on health care services and be taxable on the service portion of the premium. (NOTE: Employer-provided health care benefit would still not be taxable to the employer or employee.)

The treatment of insurance outlined above is really just like any insurance is treated today under the income tax, if you think about it. Today, insurance premiums are paid by individuals with after-tax dollars, meaning they are taxed.

Q: How are employer-provided benefits treated under the NRST?

A: Employer-provided benefits, such as pension contributions and health care plans, are not retail consumption and, therefore, are not taxed. (Pension contributions and health care benefits are taxed when they are spent on retirement living or health care services, for instance.)

In effect, the NRST maintains the deduction for employer-provided benefits.

Under the flat tax, most employer-provided benefits are not deductible.

Q: Is used property taxed?

The purchase of used property is taxable. However, an important rule of the NRST is that the government only gets to tax a good once. Therefore, HR

2001 creates a used-property tax credit. The seller of the used property gets a credit for the unconsumed value of the used good. A couple of examples to help clarify:

- A taxpayer buys a $10,000 car. For the sake of simplicity, assume a 10 percent NRST rate, making the tax due on the car equal to $1,000. If the taxpayer sells the car for $7,500 a year later, the new buyer will pay a tax of $750. Because the original owner only "consumed" $2,500 of the value of the car, he will get a credit for the unconsumed portion, or $750, which can be applied to a new car. Therefore, the government does not get to tax that same vehicle over and over again.

- This also applies to appreciating assets. Assume a taxpayer buys a $100,000 home. As explained in the Q&A on housing, a tax of $10,000 will be paid over the life of the mortgage. If the owner later sells the home for $125,000, he will receive a credit for $10,000 that can be applied to his new home.

Q: How are financial services handled?

A: Financial services pose a unique challenge to any consumer-based tax, including the flat tax, the USA tax, and the NRST.

To illustrate a simple example of this challenge, take a checking account that charges $10 a month in fees and pays five percent interest. Under the NRST, that $10 fee would be taxed. Banks would likely eliminate the fee, and lower the interest rate to three percent to compensate. The same situation applies to brokerage fees, insurance premiums, and every other financial service.

If we do not want the entire financial services sector to drop out of the tax base—which is a significant part of the economy—special rules must be developed for financial services.

Under HR 2001, any explicitly stated financial service fee (such as a checking account or brokerage fee) is taxed, as would be expected. However, an implicit financial fee is also defined and then taxed, to prevent the situation described above.

Q: How will the rights of taxpayers—especially retailers—be protected

under the NRST?

A: Our bill makes some very important reforms when it comes to taxpayer rights.

Most important, the burden of proof is shifted from the taxpayer to the government. Under the income tax today, the burden of proof is on the taxpayer to prove he does not owe a tax. Under the NRST, the burden of proof is on the government to prove that a taxpayer—either an individual or a business—does owe the tax. (The burden of document production still lies with the taxpayer, of course.)

Also, the government must pay the attorneys' and accountants' fees in any case the government can not show its case was substantially justified.

In addition, the bill creates a problem resolution office at the Department of the Treasury to investigate taxpayer complaints and stop collection activities if not in compliance with the law.

Q: How will the government collect the self-employment tax?

A: The self-employment tax, which represents the employer's share of the Social Security payroll tax for self-employed individuals, will be collected—like FICA—by the Social Security Administration.

Obviously, this is a compliance burden on the self-employed that others do not face. The legislation does, however, try to make that burden as light as possible, and rewrites the self-employment tax section of the tax code to operate in a sales tax world.

Q: How is rent treated?

A: Residential rent clearly falls in the category of a final retail good or service, and is, therefore, taxable.

Commercial rent, which is a business input, is not taxable—otherwise, the tax would simply be hidden in the cost of the final good or service produced at that location.

Q: With no IRS, what will happen to state income tax?

A: Most states with income taxes piggyback off the federal system. States generally do not have their own independent income reporting systems in place and rely on the IRS for most income data.

States will have one of two options: Either they will have to establish their own income reporting system, or they will have to convert the income tax to a sales tax base.

Our bill has language permitting states to work with each other to collect and report income data, which may or may not be legal otherwise, if they choose to stick with the income tax.

Q: **Is the purchase of collectibles taxed (i.e. artwork, jewelry, coins, etc.)?**

A: While these are generally regarded as investments, attempting to determine whether a tangible good is used for consumption or investment purposes is an administrative nightmare we don't want to get into.

However, the used-tax credit makes it work out fine.

In this context the used-property tax would work as follows:

- A painting is purchased for $1,000. If the tax rate (again for simplicity's sake) is 10 percent, a tax of $100 is paid. When the painting is sold for $2,000, the buyer pays $200 in tax. The government gets $100 and the seller gets a full $100 credit.

- The rule is that the government only gets paid a tax on the value of an item once.

- Also, "casual and isolated sales" among private parties are not taxed under $2,000 (but not more than $5,000 annually).

Q: **What will the combined state and federal tax rate be if we have to replace the state and federal income taxes? Won't the combined rate be so high that the system will be unworkable?**

A: Yes, that combined rate will be high, probably at least 20 percent, if not much higher, depending on the state.

But the fact is, this is how much the government costs our country. Government is so big that it accounts for nearly one-half of our economy.

Whether these taxes are in the form of a sales tax or not, every consumer still pays them—no matter how they are disguised. (Remember: Only consumers pay taxes, businesses simply collect taxes.)

If the taxes we pay to support this behemoth are not explicitly stated in a sales tax rate, they will be hidden in the service of every good or service we buy.

Q: How will FICA taxes be collected if income taxes and the IRS are abolished?

A: Same as today. Employers will deduct them from your paycheck (and send them to the federal Treasury) and recalculate the lower rates based on poverty-level income.

Q: What will happen to all the current IRS employees and agents?

A: Some will be needed at Treasury to manage the new state-by-state collection system for the national sales tax. Most will find new jobs in a growing private marketplace fueled by the new government policy that no longer taxes income earnings, saving, and investing.

Q: Won't a 15 percent rate encourage a black market in retail sales to avoid the tax?

A: Yes, but a growing underground market already exists to avoid income taxes. Unreported incomes, barter, cash transaction, all now cost the Treasury a loss of some $100 billion a year. We all pay higher income taxes than we should to make that up.

Our plan at least will tax that underground economy when these unreported earnings are spent—even when, for example, illegal money made in dope, prostitution, or gambling is spent, or when illegal abusers spend their unreported earnings.

Our plan also pays the retailer one-half of one percent of the sales tax to collect and send to the states. The states receive a one percent commission, too. That's about $300 million for a state like Texas. And that's a pretty good incentive to police the system well.

Automatically, a retail sales tax has fewer taxpayers than our income tax, thus, there are fewer to watch. And finally, we include strong incentives to report those who would seek to violate the law as well as exemptions for ordinary nontaxable events like garage sales.

Q: What about my home mortgage deduction? Do I get to keep it?

A: Yes. You keep it and you get even a better deal.

Current law already taxes everything made in America that goes into your home—the hidden 10-to-15 percent income tax cost. On top of that, you buy your home with "after-tax dollars," with dollars earned subject to the income tax. Thus, except for the dollars that go to pay mortgage interest you now pay taxes twice on the principal cost of your time: Income taxes up front, then hidden taxes on the purchase price.

Under our plan, you pay no income taxes. The money you spend on your house is earned, income tax free. Under our plan, the hidden 10-to-15 percent extra cost is gone, but you would pay the 15 percent sales tax, usually amortized over the life of your mortgage, and on the principal only—not on the home mortgage interest account.

We throw in two added and very attractive features.

First, our plan exempts all current purchases. So if you are currently purchasing a home at the time of enactment of the legislation, we figured you've already paid enough taxes on it. You'll be exempt.

Second, our plan provides that when you sell a home in the future upon which you have paid all or part of your sales tax, you will get a used-property tax credit on the purchase of the next home equal to the sales tax you've already paid. You will never again have to pay tax twice on the same value as you move from home to home.

Q: Won't the rich make out like bandits under a national sales tax?

A: No. Rich folks spend a lot more than po-folks, and they buy bigger and

106

more expensive toys. They will pay the same rate of sales tax—15 percent—but they will pay more of it, more often.

When Steve Forbes contested for the Republican nomination on the flat tax platform, do you remember the difficulty he had with the question about his personal tax advantage under a flat tax. Specifically, that he would pay no income taxes under his plan on his investment earnings (like those from *Forbes Magazine*), while you and I might pay the flat 20 percent on a goodly chunk of our income. He correctly pointed out that, under his plan, the business (*Forbes Magazine*) would already have paid the income tax before he earned his investment. The problem is, however, that consumers like you and me would eventually end up paying those business taxes when we make our purchase (the hidden income tax cost). We pay twice, once on our income then as a consumer, he only pays once as a consumer. He pays nothing on his earnings.

Under our national sales tax plan, when Steve Forbes buys a filet mignon steak, he pays the 15 percent sales tax just like we do when we purchase a hot dog. We both pay only once, yet he pays more tax on that filet mignon because last time I looked, it still cost more than a hot dog.

All of us at every income level will be able to decide for ourselves how much we pay in taxes by how much we spend of our income above the poverty line (below which, we are held harmless with the FICA credit). It's a good bet the rich will pay a lot more in national sales taxes than most Americans who simply couldn't afford the kind of purchases rich folks can afford. (Have you tried to buy a yacht lately?)

Q: How will the national sales tax be collected?

A: Currently 45 states collect state sales taxes. Our plan would encourage them to collect the national sales tax at the same time. Obviously that would encourage them to standardize collections. That would be great for national retailers. Remember, we provide that any retailer who sells in five or more states can deal directly with the Treasury.

Because we provide a one percent commission to the collecting state, the plan contains no "unfunded mandates." Retailers, too, are provided a one-half of one percent commission.

In the five states without a sales tax, either the state could elect to set up a collection system, contract with another state, or a federal one would be installed.

Q: **What about non-wage earners on a fixed income? Don't they get burned with a sales tax since they can't get the FICA tax credit as offset?**

A: No, for three reasons. First, our plan eliminates the hidden 10-to-15 percent income tax cost in all their purchases. Thus, the 15 percent sales tax is likely a near wash. But most fixed income individuals are on some form of COLA-adjusted pension, Social Security, government, or private pension plan. If there isn't a complete wash in the switch in taxes and prices do rise, the COLA adjustment compensates for that rise.

Obviously, the problem is more difficult for a non-COLA adjusted pension, and we are frankly exploring different alternative adjustments. We do not intend to increase such a person's tax on the lower income end of our economy. Our goal is to end the double and currently regressive taxation on those incomes. We have included a COLA rebate plan for those pensioners.

And there is a third, and perhaps more important, benefit to fixed income persons in America with the national sales tax. Under our current oppressive income tax structure, which paralyzes American jobs, income, savings, and investment, we are down to three working Americans for every one retired. By the early years of the fast-approaching new century, we'll be down to two working Americans for every one person who is retired. Keeping Medicare and Social Security afloat will require a doubling of current payroll taxes on those unlucky enough to be carrying the load. At that point, you begin to see our social support systems collapsing.

The solution lies in creating more and better jobs, in giving workers more incentives to earn and investors more incentive to invest in those American jobs. The very best solution lies is ending the trade deficit with a program that gives American-made products a chance to compete in world trade, both here and abroad.

The national sales tax plan rewards income and investment and, thus, helps create jobs. By ending the hidden income tax disadvantage on American-made products, it brings manufacturing jobs back to America and helps reduce the trade deficit. That creates new and higher-paying American jobs. And that is ultimately the single most important thing we can do for those on fixed pensions who must depend upon the support of wage earners.

Q: Will the national sales tax apply only to retail sales?

A: Yes, the NRST is collected only at the retail sales level to the final consumer. For example, no tax is collected on sales for resale. No tax is collected on wholesale transactions. No tax is collected on purchases made of items used in making or manufacturing finished products. There is no manufacturing or value-added tax. The plan calls for the tax to be paid by the consumer, collected by the retailer and remitted to the state government, which manages the system in the state and then forwards the collection to the Treasury.

Q: Does the national sales tax apply to goods only?

A: No. The tax applies to the retail consumption of both goods and services, with the limited exemption for education tuition. Thus, the 15 percent tax is applied to typical professional services, such as legal, accounting, and medical services. But remember under our plan, the professional provider, lawyer, accountant, or doctor is exempt from income taxes, and the money we used to pay those services is also exempt from income taxes. We, thus, can better afford the service, and the providers have room, if they choose, to lower their rates, since they will owe no income tax on those fees. There is, of course, no practical way to require them to do so. The marketplace will or will not produce those results. Wise consumers can make sure it happens.

Q: Are there any exemptions from the national sales tax on food and drugs?

A: No. But food and drug purchases made with income earned up to the poverty level are actually sales tax free, because the sales tax collected on all income up to the poverty line is returned to the wage-earning taxpayer through lower FICA tax withholding on each paycheck. For non-wage earners, the COLA increase on Social Security and other pension funds compensates for any increase caused in the price of food and drugs. For non-COLA adjusted pensions, we have included a COLA rebate plan.

Remember also that the cost of most food and drug items will be reduced by the repeal of the 10-to-15 percent hidden income tax cost. In a competitive environment, some, if not all, of those cost savings get passed on to consumers. With the FICA rebate, many wage earners will actually be dollars ahead on their food and drug purchases.

Q: Isn't it unfair to charge a national sales tax on purchases I make with savings that I've already paid income tax on?

A: Yes, but that's what happens today with the IRS. You now pay income taxes first. Then as a consumer, you pay all the hidden business income tax cost (10-to-15 percent) that goes into the price of everything made in America. Only when you buy foreign do you escape this double taxation, and that's not a very good message.

Under our plan, double taxation is avoided on new income, including new interest on your savings, and even on old income that was previously taxed up to the poverty line for your family size (because of the reduced FICA withholding) if you are a current wage earner.

If you are not a current wage earner, we at least get rid of the hidden IRS (10-to-15 percent) tax on American-made products you consume, and we have added a Social Security benefit to protect retirement income. We are currently examining transition rules for prior savings.

Q: Will there be a transition period for the repeal of the IRS and income tax and the implementation of the national sales tax?

A: Yes, there must be a transition period. How long and how it will work must be carefully constructed. Moving from one system to the other too quickly would probably cause economic dislocation and would unfairly treat those who have made financial decisions on the basis of the current tax code. People will need (and deserve) time to adjust. Moving too slowly would probably lose some of the potential economic effects of the shift from income to consumption taxation. The transition will need to be resolutely carried out over a reasonable and clearly defined time period.

Q: Is there an exemption for charitable giving?

A: Charitable donations are not taxed, because only money that is spent is taxed. There is, however, no special treatment for purchases at retail made by charitable, religious, or other nonprofits. All purchases of goods at retail are taxed.

Q: Will the repeal of the income tax end the tax advantage for certain investments, like tax-free municipal bonds?

A: Yes, because investment becomes tax free. Municipal bonds, like all financing, would compete for investors' dollars, but in a market where income is not taxed from any source. Government issues, of course, can still have the advantage of "full faith and credit" guarantees.

Q: Are advertisements subject to the NRST?

A: No, if they are business advertisements, since these ads are simply part of the marketing costs. The NRST is applied when advertised products are actually purchased for nonbusiness purposes, *i.e.*, a classified ad.

Q: Will government purchases be subject to the national sales tax?

A: Yes, all purchases at retail for consumption are taxed, including those made by local, state, and federal government agencies. Also taxed by the NRST are state and local services that are provided in competition with free-market entities, to insure that government entities do not unfairly compete with workers and businesses in the private sector.

Q: Are education expenses taxable under the NRST?

A: No, tuition for educational or job training is not taxed under the NRST. Other purchases, books, rents, etc., are.

Q: What about self-employed wage earners? Will they have to continue to file some kind of income report for self-employment FICA taxes?

A: Yes, and all employers will still be required to file a FICA report on each employee. Treasury will manage the system of FICA rebates (reduced FICA withholding) for wage earners up to the poverty line. But there will be no income tax forms, no estimated tax forms, no income tax withholding. The IRS will be abolished. April 15 will truly be just another day in our lives.

111

APPENDIX B

Top Ten List

Finally, here are my Top Ten serious reasons for repealing both the federal income tax and the IRS:

10. End all payroll income tax withholdings.
9. Give every income taxpaying citizen an immediate and substantial increase in take home pay equal to income taxes formerly withheld.
8. Save $300 billion each year in filing and compliance costs.
7. End double taxation.
6. End the federal government's role in deciding how we should earn, spend, save, or invest our income, expanding personal freedoms.
5. Terminate the current incentive for us to "buy foreign."
4. End the authority of the IRS (and its 120,000 agents), the most intrusive agency in America.
3. No more "you are guilty, until proven innocent."
2. No more IRS audits.
1. Make April 15 just another pleasant springtime day in our lives.

And my Top Ten less serious reasons are:

10. Let the income tax replace the Black Plague as history's darkest moment.
9. The letters IRS can be used for some new nicer federal agency. (How about, for instance, the Infant Relief Service.)
8. Make Willie Nelson a happy man.
7. Get rid of a "lien" and "very mean" IRS.
6. Make the CIA the toughest kid on the block again.
5. Get Steve Forbes to talk about something else—anything else!
4. Make Whitewater legal.
3. End the marriage penalty—marriage has enough penalties.
2. Make golf our best reason to lie again.
1. No longer will telling "the truth, the whole truth and nothing but the truth" mean three different things in Washington, D.C.

APPENDIX C

Do You Want To Know More?

For further information on HR 2001, the National Retail Sales Tax, please visit:
www.house.gov/tauzin

For further information on HR 1040, the Armey Flat Tax, please visit:
www.flattax.house.gov

Additional Information Is Available From:

Citizens for an Alternative Tax System
www.cats.org
(1-800-767-7577)

Citizens for a Sound Economy
www.cse.org
(1-800-JOIN-CSE)

APPENDIX D

National Retail Sales Act 1997

H. R. 2001

105th CONGRESS

1st Session

H. R. 2001

To promote freedom, fairness, and economic opportunity for families by repealing the income tax, abolishing the Internal Revenue Service, and enacting a national retail sales tax to be administered primarily by the States.

IN THE HOUSE OF REPRESENTATIVES

June 19, 1997

Mr. DAN SCHAEFER of Colorado (for himself, Mr. TAUZIN, Mr. BONO, Mr. HALL of Texas, Mr. HEFLEY, Mr. LINDER, Mrs. MYRICK, Mr. NORWOOD, Mr. PACKARD, Mr. STUMP, and Mr. WICKER) introduced the following bill; which was referred to the Committee on Ways and Means

---

A BILL

To promote freedom, fairness, and economic opportunity for families by repealing the income tax, abolishing the Internal Revenue Service, and enacting a national retail sales tax to be administered primarily by the States.

Be it enacted by the Senate and House of Representatives of the United States of America in Congress assembled,

SECTION 1. SHORT TITLE; TABLE OF CONTENTS.

(a) SHORT TITLE- This Act may be cited as the `National Retail Sales Tax Act of 1997'.

(b) TABLE OF CONTENTS- The table of contents of this Act is as follows:

Chapter 1--Sales Tax

`SUBCHAPTER A--IMPOSITION OF TAX

`SUBCHAPTER B--CREDITS; REFUNDS; INSTALLMENT PAYMENTS OF TAX ON PURCHASES OF RESIDENCES

`SUBCHAPTER C--DEFINITIONS AND SPECIAL RULES; FINANCIAL INTERMEDIATION SERVICES

`SUBCHAPTER D--AUTHORITY FOR STATES TO COLLECT TAX

SEC. 2. CONGRESSIONAL FINDINGS.

(a) The Congress finds that the income tax--

(1) retards economic growth and has reduced the standard of living of the American public;

(2) impedes the international competitiveness of United States industry;

(3) reduces savings and investment in the United States;

(4) lowers productivity;

(5) imposes unacceptable administrative costs on taxpayers, individuals and businesses alike;

(6) is unfair and inequitable; and

(7) unnecessarily intrudes upon the privacy and civil rights of United States citizens.

(b) The Congress finds further that national sales, services and use tax on final consumption of goods and services--

(1) is similar in many respects to those in place in 45 of the 50 States;

(2) will promote savings;

(3) will promote fairness;

(4) will promote economic growth;

(5) will raise the standard of living;

(6) will increase savings and investment;

(7) will enhance productivity and international competitiveness;

(8) will reduce administrative burdens on the taxpayer; and

(9) will respect the privacy interests and civil rights of taxpayers.

(c) The Congress further finds that--

(1) most of the practical experience administering sales taxes is found at the State Governmental level;

(2) it is desirable to harmonize Federal and State collection and enforcement efforts to the maximum extent possible;

(3) it is sound tax administration policy to administer and collect the Federal sales and service tax at the State level in return for a reasonable administration fee to the States;

(4) businesses that must collect and remit taxes should receive reasonable compensation for the cost of doing so; and

(5) the sixteenth amendment to the Constitution should be repealed.

SEC. 3. REPEAL OF THE INCOME TAX, ESTATE AND GIFT TAXES, AND CERTAIN EXCISE TAXES.

(a) IN GENERAL- The following provisions of the Internal Revenue Code of 1986 are hereby repealed:

(1) Chapter 1 (relating to income tax).

(2) Chapter 5 (relating to tax on transfers to avoid income tax).

(3) Chapter 6 (relating to consolidated returns).

(4) Chapter 24 (relating to collection of income tax at source).

(5) Subtitle B (relating to estate and gift taxes).

(6) Chapter 31 (relating to retail excise taxes).

(7) Chapter 32 (relating to manufacturers excise taxes).

(8) Subtitle E (relating to alcohol, tobacco, and certain other excise taxes).

(9) Subtitle F (relating to procedure and administration of the income tax and certain other taxes) except for section 6103 (relating to confidentiality), chapter 66 (relating to limitations), chapter 67 (relating to interest), section 6656 (relating to failure to make deposit of taxes), section 6657 (relating to bad checks), section 6658 (relating to coordination with title 11), chapter 75 (relating to crimes), chapter 76 (relating to Judicial Proceedings), section 7431 (relating to damages for unauthorized disclosure), section 7432 (relating to damages for failure to release lien), section 7433 (relating to damages for unauthorized collection data) and chapter 77 (relating to miscellaneous provisions). References to provisions repealed by the preceding sentence shall be treated as references to such provisions as in effect on the day before the date of the enactment of this Act.

(b) EFFECTIVE DATE-

(1) IN GENERAL- Except as provided in paragraph (2), the amendments

made by subsection (a) shall take effect on July 1, 1999.

(2) INCOME TAX- The amendment made by subsection (a)(1) shall apply to taxable years beginning after June 30, 1999.

(3) SALES TAX- The amendment made by section 4 shall take effect on July 1, 1999.

(4) SOCIAL SECURITY BENEFITS- The amendment made by section 9 shall take effect on January 1, 1999.

(5) SUPERMAJORITY REQUIRED- The amendment made by section 11 shall take effect on January 1, 1999.

SEC. 4. SALES TAX.

Subtitle A of the Internal Revenue Code of 1986 is amended by inserting at the beginning the following new chapter:

`CHAPTER 1--SALES TAX

`SUBCHAPTER A. Imposition of tax.

`SUBCHAPTER B. Credits; refunds; installment payments of tax on purchases of residences.

`SUBCHAPTER C. Definitions and special rules; financial intermediation services.

`SUBCHAPTER D. Authority for States to collect tax.

`SUBCHAPTER E. Other administrative provisions.

`Subchapter A--Imposition of Tax

`Sec. 1. Imposition of tax.

`Sec. 2. Exemptions.

`Sec. 3. Special rules relating to collection and remittance of tax.

`SECTION 1. IMPOSITION OF TAX.

`(a) IN GENERAL- There is hereby imposed a tax of 15 percent on the gross payments for the use, consumption or enjoyment in the United States of any taxable property or service, whether produced or rendered within or without the United States.

`(b) COORDINATION WITH IMPORT DUTIES- The taxes imposed by this section are in addition to any import duties imposed by law. The Secretary shall provide by regulation that, to the maximum extent practicable, the taxes imposed by this section on imported property and services are collected and administered in conjunction with any applicable import duties.

`(c) LIABILITY FOR COLLECTION AND REMITTANCE OF THE TAX-

  `(1) GENERAL RULE- The tax imposed by subsection (a) shall be collected and remitted by the seller, except as provided in subsection (2).

  `(2) TAX TO BE PAID BY PURCHASER IN CERTAIN CIRCUMSTANCES-

    `(A) GENERAL RULE- In the case of taxable property or services purchased outside of the United States for use, consumption or enjoyment in the United States, the purchaser shall remit the tax imposed by subsection (a).

    `(B) In the case of a purchaser electing to pay tax in installments pursuant to section 12, the purchaser shall remit the tax imposed by subsection (a).

    `(C) Employers that pay wages that are taxable services within the meaning of section 21(n) shall be responsible for paying and remitting the tax.

    `(D) The Secretary may provide by regulation that the tax imposed by subsection (a) is to be collected and remitted by the purchaser rather than the seller.

`SEC. 2. EXEMPTIONS.

`(a) IN GENERAL- Except as provided in section 3(b)(2), no tax shall be imposed under section 1 on any taxable property or service purchased for--

  `(1) a business purpose in an active trade or business, or

  `(2) export from the United States for use or consumption outside the United States, provided that the purchaser provided the seller with--

    `(A) an intermediate sales certificate, or

    `(B) an export sales certificate.

`(b) BUSINESS PURPOSES- For purposes of this section, the term `purchased for a business purpose in an active trade or business' means purchased by a person engaged in an active trade or business and used in that active trade or business--

  `(1) for resale,

  `(2) to produce taxable property or services (as defined in section 21(e)), or

  `(3) in furtherance of other bona fide business purposes.

`(c) DE MINIMIS PAYMENTS- Up to $400 of gross payments per calendar year--

`(1) made by a person not engaged in an active trade or business at any time during such calendar year prior to making such gross payments, and

`(2) made to purchase any taxable property or service which is imported into the United States by such person for use or consumption by such person in the United States,

shall be exempt from the tax imposed by section 1.

`(d) DE MINIMIS SALES- Up to $2,500 per calendar year of gross payments received--

`(1) by a person not engaged in an active trade or business during such calendar year prior to the receipt of such gross payments, and

`(2) in connection with a casual or isolated sale,

shall be exempt from the tax imposed by section 1.

`(e) AFFILIATED FIRMS- Firms that make purchases from or sell to affiliated firms which are exempt pursuant to subsection (a) shall not need to comply with the requirements of subsection (g) for such purchases to remain exempt. For purposes of this section, a firm is affiliated with another if 1 firm owns 50 percent of the voting shares or interest in the other.

`(f) DE MINIMIS SALE OF FINANCIAL INTERMEDIATION SERVICES- The first $10,000 per calendar year of gross payments received by a person from the sale of financial intermediation services shall be exempt from the tax imposed by section 1. The exemption provided by this subsection is in addition to other exemptions afforded by this chapter.

`(g) SELLER RELIEVED OF LIABILITY IN CERTAIN CASES- In the case of any property or service which is sold exempt from tax pursuant to subsection (a), if the seller--

`(1) has on file a copy of an exemption certificate (whether an intermediate sale or export sale certificate) from the purchaser, and

`(2) did not have reasonable cause to believe that an exemption from the tax imposed by section 1 was unavailable to the purchaser with respect to such purchase, then the seller shall be relieved of liability to collect and remit the tax imposed by section 1 on such purchase.

`SEC. 3. RULES RELATING TO COLLECTION AND REMITTANCE OF TAX.

`(a) OBLIGATION OF GOVERNMENTAL UNITS AND NOT-FOR-PROFIT ORGANIZATIONS TO COLLECT, REMIT AND PAY TAXES-

`(1) GOVERNMENTAL UNITS- Nothing in this subtitle shall be construed to exempt any Federal, State, or local governmental unit or political subdivision from paying any tax imposed by this subtitle on any sale, purchase, use, consumption or enjoyment by such a unit.

`(2) NOT-FOR-PROFIT ORGANIZATIONS-

`(A) IN GENERAL- Dues, contributions and payments to qualified not-for-profit organizations shall not be considered gross payments for taxable property or services for purposes of this subtitle.

`(B) EXCEPTION- Notwithstanding subparagraph (2)(A), payments of any form to a qualified not-for-profit organization shall be considered gross payments for taxable property or services unless said organization establishes that the property or service provided in exchange is--

`(i) substantially related to the purposes of the qualified not-for-profit organization, or

`(ii) is not commercially available.

`(C) For purposes of this section, qualified not-for-profit organization means a not-for-profit organization organized and operated exclusively--

`(i) for religious, charitable, scientific, testing for public safety, literary or educational purposes;

`(ii) as civic leagues or social welfare organizations;

`(iii) as labor, agricultural or horticultural organizations;

`(iv) as chambers of commerce, business leagues or trade associations; or

`(v) as fraternal beneficiary societies, orders or associations;

no part of the net earnings of which inures to the benefit of any private shareholder or individual.

`(D) Upon application in a form prescribed by the State Administrator, the State Administrator shall provide qualification certificates to qualified not-for-profit organizations.

`(E) If a not-for-profit organization provides taxable property or services in connection with contributions or dues to the organizations, then it shall be required to treat the provision of said taxable property or services as a purchase taxable pursuant to this subtitle at the fair market value of said property or personal services.

`(F) Taxable property and services purchased by not-for-profit organizations for resale or for use in the production of taxable property or services shall be eligible for the exemptions provided in section 2.

`(b) TAX COLLECTED ON CERTAIN EXEMPT PURCHASES-

`(1) IN GENERAL- In the case of a purchase which would (but for this subsection (b)) be exempt from the tax imposed by section 1 by reason of section 2(a), such subsection shall not apply to such purchase if the seller--

`(A) elects the application of this subsection, and

`(B) immediately provides the purchaser with a receipt reflecting the information required by section 54. Seller may elect to exercise the application of this section with respect to some or all purchases or purchasers.

`(2) The Secretary may by regulation provide that certain industries or specific products are such that the vendor must collect the tax on otherwise exempt purchases if, in the Secretary's judgment, said industry or products are such that consumers buy 25 percent or more of the product sold by the industry or the product. A registered vendor may by application for good cause shown elect to opt out of the application of this paragraph.

`(3) CROSS REFERENCE-

`For credit to purchaser where seller collects tax on exempt purchase, see section 11(a)(3).

`For tax to be separately stated and charged, see section 54.

`(c) GOVERNMENT ENTERPRISES-

`(1) GOVERNMENT ENTERPRISES TO COLLECT AND REMIT TAXES ON SALES- Nothing in this subtitle shall be construed to exempt any Federal, State, or local governmental unit or political subdivision (whether or not the State is a conforming State) operating a government enterprise from collecting and remitting tax imposed by this subtitle on any sale of taxable property or services. Government enterprises shall comply with all duties imposed on private enterprises by this subtitle and shall be liable for penalties and subject to enforcement action in the same manner as private enterprises.

`(2) GOVERNMENT ENTERPRISE- Any entity owned or operated by a Federal, State, or local governmental unit or political subdivision that receives gross payments from selling taxable property or services to private persons is a government enterprise, provided, however, that a government-owned entity shall not become a government enterprise for purposes of this section unless in any quarter it has revenues from the sale of taxable property or services that exceed $2,500.

`(3) GOVERNMENT ENTERPRISES' INTERMEDIATE AND EXPORT SALES-

> `(A) Government enterprises shall not be subject to tax on purchases that would not be subject to tax pursuant to section 2 if the government enterprise were a private enterprise.

> `(B) Government enterprises may not use the exemption afforded by section 2 to serve as a conduit for tax-free purchases by government units that would otherwise be subject to taxation on purchases pursuant to section 1. Transfers of taxable property or services purchased exempt from tax by a government enterprise to such government unit shall be taxable.

`(4) SEPARATE BOOKS OF ACCOUNT- Any government enterprise must maintain books of account, separate from the nonenterprise government accounts, maintained in accordance with generally accepted accounting principles.

`(5) ACTIVE TRADE OR BUSINESS- A government enterprise shall be treated as an active trade or business.

`(6) CROSS REFERENCE-

> `For obligation of government units, see section 3(a)(1).

`Subchapter B--Credits; Refunds; Installment Payments of Tax on Purchases of Residences

`Sec. 11. Credits and refunds.

`Sec. 12. Installment payments of tax on purchases of principal residences.

`Sec. 13. Family Consumption Refund.

`SEC. 11. CREDITS AND REFUNDS.

`(a) GENERAL CREDITS- Each person shall be allowed a credit against the taxes imposed by section 1 for any month in an amount equal to the sum of--

> `(1) such person's used property credit under subsection (c) for such month,

> `(2) such person's business use conversion credit under subsection (d) for such month,

> `(3) the amount paid by such person with respect to a purchase during such month by reason of a tax collected on an exempt purchase pursuant to section 3(b) (relating to election to collect tax on certain nontaxable purchases),

`(4) the administration credit under section (e),

`(5) the compliance equipment cost credit under section (f),

`(6) the bad debt credit under subsection (g),

`(7) the insurance proceeds credit under subsection (h),

`(8) the transition inventory credit under subsection (i), and

`(9) any amount paid in excess of amount due.

`(b) REFUNDS-

`(1) FILERS- If a person files two consecutive monthly tax reports with a credit balance, then, upon application in a form prescribed by the State Administrator, then the credit balance shown on the second monthly report shall be refunded to the taxpayer within 60 days of said application.

`(2) NONFILERS- If a person other than a monthly filer has an excess credit for any month, then, upon application in a form prescribed by the State Administrator, then the credit balance due shall be refunded to the taxpayer within 60 days of said application.

`(3) INTEREST- No interest shall be required to be paid on any overpayment under this subsection for any month if such overpayment is paid within 60 days after the close of such month.

`(4) SUSPENSION OF PERIOD TO PAY REFUND ONLY IF FEDERAL COURT RULING- The 60-day periods under paragraphs (1) and (2) shall be suspended with respect to a purported credit balance (or portion thereof) only during any period that there is in effect a preliminary ruling from a Federal court that there is reasonable cause to believe that such credit balance is not actually the amount due.

`(5) FILER- For purposes of this subsection, the term `filer' means, with respect to any month, any person required to register under section 43 for such month.

`(c) USED PROPERTY CREDIT-

`(1) IN GENERAL- For purposes of subsection (a), a seller shall receive credit for previous sales tax paid on the resale of taxable property or services, as provided in this subsection (c).

`(2) DETERMINATION OF USED PROPERTY CREDIT AMOUNT- The used property credit amount determined under this paragraph with respect to any property is the lesser of--

`(A) the amount of tax due and paid by virtue of the present transaction (without regard to any credits), or

`(B) the most recent prior tax imposed by section 1 with respect to such property transaction (without regard to any credits).

`(3) TRANSITIONAL DEEMED PAID RULE FOR PROPERTY OWNED ON EFFECTIVE DATE OF ACT- In the case of property which was acquired by the seller before July 1, 1999, the amount under paragraph (2)(B) shall be the amount which is the product of--

`(A) that which would be determined under paragraph (2)(B) as if this subtitle had been in effect at the time of such acquisition, and

`(B) the equity ratio (as defined in paragraph (4)).

`(4) The equity ratio is the quotient of--

`(A) the income tax basis in the property at the end of the taxable year 1999, less the mortgage or debt secured by said property at the end of said taxable year, divided by

`(B) the income tax basis in the property at the end of the taxable year 1999,

provided, however, that the quantity defined in subparagraph (1) cannot be less than zero and further

providing that the equity ratio so calculated cannot be less than zero or greater than one.

`(d) Business Use Conversion Credit-

`(1) IN GENERAL- For purposes of subsection (a), a person's business use conversion credit for any month is the aggregate of the amounts determined under paragraph (2) with respect to property--

`(A) on which a prior tax was imposed by section 1 on the purchase by such person, and

`(B) which commences to be exclusively used during such month in the production by such person of other taxable property or services.

`(2) AMOUNT OF CREDIT- The amount determined under this paragraph with respect to any property is lesser of--

`(A) the product of the rate imposed by section 1 and the fair market value of the property when its use is converted, and

`(B) the prior tax referred to in paragraph (1)(A).

`(3) Property converted from business use to personal use shall be subject to tax pursuant to section 1 on the book value of the converted property as of the date of conversion, provided that the books are kept in accordance with generally accepted accounting principles.

`(e) ADMINISTRATION CREDIT- Every taxpayer filing a timely monthly report in compliance with section 41 shall be entitled to a taxpayer administrative credit equal to the greater of--

`(1) $200, or

`(2) one-half of 1 percent of the tax remitted, provided, however, that in no event will the credit afforded by this section exceed 20 percent of the tax due to be remitted prior to the application of this credit.

`(f) COMPLIANCE EQUIPMENT COST CREDIT- Vendors required to purchase new equipment to comply with the provisions of section 54 shall be entitled to a credit in the amount of 50 percent of the cost of such equipment.

`(g) BAD DEBT CREDIT-

`(1) FINANCIAL INTERMEDIATION SERVICES- Any person registered pursuant to section 43 who has experienced a bad debt (other than unpaid invoices within the meaning of paragraph (2)) shall be entitled to a credit equal to the product of--

`(A) the rate imposed by section 1, and

`(B) the quotient that is--

`(i) the amount of the bad debt (as defined in section 24), divided by

`(ii) the quantity that is 1 minus the rate imposed by section 1.

`(2) UNPAID INVOICES- Any person electing the accrual method pursuant to section 56 that has with respect to a transaction--

`(A) invoiced the tax imposed by section 1,

`(B) remitted the invoiced tax,

`(C) actually delivered the taxable property or performed the taxable services invoiced, and

`(D) not been paid 90 days after the date the invoice was due to be paid,

shall be entitled to a credit equal to the amount of tax remitted and unpaid by the purchaser.

`(3) SUBSEQUENT PAYMENT- Any payment made with respect to a transaction subsequent to a subsection (g) credit being taken with respect to that transaction shall be subject to tax in the month the payment was received as if a tax inclusive sale of taxable property and services in the amount of the payment had been made.

`(4) PARTIAL PAYMENTS- Partial payments shall be treated as pro rata payments of the underlying obligation and shall be allocated proportionately among payment for the taxable property and service, tax and otherwise (in the case of partially nontaxable payments).

`(5) RELATED PARTIES- The credit provided by this section shall not be available with respect to sales made to affiliated firms (within the meaning of section 2(e)).

`(h) INSURANCE PROCEEDS CREDIT-

`(1) IN GENERAL- A person receiving a payment from an insurer by virtue of an insurance contract shall be entitled to a credit in an amount determined by paragraph (2), less any amount paid to the insured by the insurer pursuant to paragraph (3), if the entire premium (except that portion allocable to the investment account of the underlying policy) for the insurance contract giving rise to the insurer's obligation to make a payment to the insured was subject to the tax imposed by section 1 and such tax was paid.

`(2) CREDIT AMOUNT- The amount of the credit shall be the product of--

   `(A) the rate imposed by section 1, and

   `(B) the quotient that is--

      `(i) the amount of the payment made by the insurer to the insured, divided by

      `(ii) the quantity that is 1 minus the rate imposed by section 1.

`(3) ADMINISTRATIVE OPTION- The credit determined in accordance with paragraph (2) shall be paid by the insurer to the insured and the insurer shall be entitled to the credit in lieu of the insured provided, however, the insurer may elect, in a form prescribed by the Secretary, to not pay the credit and require the insured to make application for the credit. In the event of such election, the insurer shall provide to the Secretary and the insured the name and tax identification number of the insurer and of the insured and indicate the proper amount of the credit.

`(4) COORDINATION WITH RESPECT TO EXEMPTION- If taxable property or services purchased by an insurer on behalf of an insured are purchased free of tax by virtue of section 21(e)(3), then the credit provided by this section shall not be available with respect to that purchase.

`(5) INSURANCE CONTRACT- For purposes of paragraph (1), the term `insurance contract' includes a life insurance contract, a health insurance contract, a property and casualty loss insurance contract, a general liability insurance contract, a marine insurance contract, a fire insurance contract, an accident insurance contract, a disability insurance contract, a long-term care insurance contract, and an insurance contract that provides a combination of these types of insurance.

`(i) TRANSITIONAL INVENTORY CREDIT-

`(1) TRANSITION INVENTORY CREDIT- A credit shall be allowed equal to the product of the rate of tax imposed by section 1 and the cost of qualified inventory.

`(2) INVENTORY-

`(A) QUALIFIED INVENTORY- Inventory held by an active trade or business on the close of business June 30, 1999, that is subsequently sold subject to the tax imposed by section 1 shall be qualified inventory.

`(B) COST- For purposes of this section, qualified inventory shall have the cost that it had on the income tax return of the active trade or business filed for the period ending June 30, 1999 (including any amounts capitalized by virtue of section 263A as in effect on June 30, 1999).

`(3) TIMING OF CREDIT- The credit provided under paragraph (1) shall be allowed on the sales tax return where the taxable sale of the qualified inventory is reported. The person claiming such credit shall attach supporting schedules in the form that the Secretary may prescribe.

`SEC. 12. INSTALLMENT PAYMENTS OF TAX ON PURCHASE OF PRINCIPAL RESIDENCES.

`(a) IN GENERAL- If--

`(1) property is purchased and used as the principal residence of any purchaser of such property, and

`(2) such purchaser elects the application of this section, then the tax imposed by section 1 with respect to such purchase shall be paid in equal annual installments over the 30-year period beginning on the date of such sale together with simple interest at the rate imposed by section 6621.

`(b) Termination of Installments if Property Is Sold or Otherwise Ceases To Be Principal Residence-

`(1) IN GENERAL- If, before the close of the 30-year period referred to in subsection (a), any property to which an election under subsection (a) applies--

`(A) is sold, or

`(B) otherwise ceases to be used as the principal residence of any purchaser making such election,

then the unpaid installments shall be due no later than two years after the time of such sale or cessation. To the extent that such sale or cessation is only of a portion of such residential property, the preceding sentence shall apply only to a like portion (based on value) of such unpaid installments.

`(2) SPECIAL RULE- In a case to which paragraph (1)(B) applies with respect to any purchaser--

`(A) if such purchaser purchases within two years another property which property is purchased and used as the principal residence of such purchaser, the remaining unpaid installments shall be due at the time of such purchase,

`(B) if subparagraph (A) does not apply to such purchaser, the remaining unpaid installments shall be due at the close of the two-year

period beginning on the date of the cessation referred to in paragraph (1); and

`(C) the two-year period referred to in subparagraph (B) shall be suspended during any period that such purchaser uses such property as his principal residence.

`(3) If any purchaser exercises the right to installment payments under this section, then the responsibility to remit the tax due is the purchaser's rather than the seller's provided that the seller has on file a copy of the election form prescribed by the Secretary.

`SEC. 13. FAMILY CONSUMPTION REFUND.

`(a) GENERAL RULE- Each qualified family unit (as defined in subsection (b)) shall be eligible to receive a sales tax rebate in an amount no greater than the product of--

`(1) the rate of tax imposed by section 1, and

`(2) the lesser of--

`(A) the poverty level (as defined in subsection (c)), or

`(B) the wage income of the family unit,

in the manner prescribed and subject to the limitations set forth by this section.

`(b) QUALIFIED FAMILY UNIT DEFINED- For purposes of this section, the term qualified family unit shall mean any family sharing a common residence. Any family members (as defined in subsection (e)) sharing a common residence shall be considered part of one integrated family unit.

`(c) POVERTY LEVEL DEFINED- The poverty level shall be the quotient that is--

`(1) the level determined by the Department of Health and Human Services poverty guidelines required by sections 652 and 673(2) of the Omnibus Reconciliation Act of 1981 (all States and the District of Columbia) for family units of a particular size, divided by

`(2) the quantity that is one minus the tax rate imposed by section 1.

`(d) REBATE MECHANISM-

`(1) GENERAL RULE- The rebate provided by section (a) shall be provided to each qualified family unit by including the pay period rebate amount in each paycheck.

`(2) PAY PERIOD REBATE AMOUNT- The pay period rebate amount shall be the lesser of product of the rate of tax imposed by the section 1 and

`(A) the wages paid during the pay period, or

`(B) the quotient that is the poverty level for the family unit (determined in accordance with subsection (c)) divided by the number of pay periods in a year.

`(3) ADJUSTED WITHHOLDING TABLES TO BE PROVIDED TO EMPLOYERS- The Social Security Administration shall publish revised withholding tables for use by employers.

`(4) COORDINATION- The family member receiving the family consumption rebate shall set forth, in a form prescribed by the Social Security Administration, the names and Social Security numbers of all members of the family unit for which a rebate is claimed. Employers shall provide this information in the form prescribed to the Social Security Administration.

`(e) FAMILY MEMBERS DEFINED- For purposes of determining the size of the family unit, family members shall include each spouse or the head of household, children, grandchildren, parents and grandparents.

`(f) DISQUALIFIED FAMILY MEMBERS- In order for a family member to be counted for purposes of determining family unit size, said family member must--

`(1) if over the age of two years, have a bona fide Social Security number; and

`(2) be a lawful resident of the United States.

`(g) STUDENTS LIVING AWAY FROM HOME- A student during each of five months in a calendar year living away from the common residence of a family unit but who receives over 50 percent of his support from the family unit shall be included as part of that family unit for purposes of this section.

`(h) CHANGE IN FAMILY CIRCUMSTANCES- The residence of family members, marital status and number of persons in a family unit on the first day of the calendar year shall govern determinations required to be made under this section for purposes of said calendar year.

`(i) TWO OR MORE FAMILY MEMBERS WORKING- The family unit may elect to divide the rebate between two family members. Family members shall make this election in a form prescribed by the Social Security Administration and shall when making said election disclose the name and Social Security number of the other family members. Creditable wages for families making this election shall not exceed one half of the poverty level for that family unit.

`(j) EMPLOYERS TO ADJUST REMITTANCES- Employers shall reduce their payroll tax remittances to the

Social Security Administration by the amount of Family Consumption Rebate provided in employee paychecks.

`(k) NO DOUBLE COUNTING- In no event shall any person be considered part of more than one family unit.

`(l) SOCIAL SECURITY ADMINISTRATION- The Social Security Administration shall provide to multiple wage-earner family units who received a lower rebate amount than that to which that were entitled under subsection (a) due to the application of the limitations in subsection (d)(2) and subsection (i) any payment due within 30 days of the close of the calendar year.

`Subchapter C--Definitions and Special Rules; Financial Intermediation Services

`Sec. 21. Definitions.

`Sec. 22. Special rules.

`Sec. 23. Determination of financial intermediation services amount.

`Sec. 24. Bad debts.

`Sec. 25. Timing of tax on financial intermediation services.

`Sec. 26. Alternative method for calculating tax due.

`Sec. 27. Basic interest rate.

`Sec. 28. Applicable interest rate.

`SEC. 21. DEFINITIONS.

`(a) FINANCIAL INTERMEDIATION SERVICES- The term `financial intermediation services' means financial intermediation services determined in accordance with section 23.

`(b) GROSS PAYMENTS- For purposes of this subtitle, the term `gross payments' shall mean gross payments inclusive of Federal tax imposed by, and State taxes imposed in conformity with, this chapter but exclusive of customs duties. Gross payment shall be the product of the pre-tax factor and the payments for the taxable property or service exclusive of State and Federal taxes imposed by, and State taxes imposed in conformity with, this subtitle. For purposes of this section, the pre-tax factor shall be one divided by the quantity that is one minus the sum of--

`(1) the Federal tax rate imposed by section 1, and

`(2) the State tax rate imposed in conformity with this subtitle.

`(c) Primary residence shall mean residential real property used predominantly as the place of abode for a person or persons. A person shall have only one primary residence for purposes of this section. A married couple shall have only one primary residence.

`(d) PURCHASED FOR RESALE- For purposes of section 2(b)(1), a property or service is purchased for resale if such property or service is purchased by a person in an active trade or business for the purpose of reselling the taxable property or service in the ordinary course of that active trade or business.

`(e) PURCHASED TO PRODUCE TAXABLE PROPERTY OR SERVICES- For purposes of section 2(b)(2)--

`(1) IN GENERAL- A property or service is purchased to produce a taxable property or service if such property or service is purchased by a person in an active trade or business for the purpose of employing or using such property or service in the production or sale of other taxable property or services in the ordinary course of that active trade or business.

`(2) RESEARCH EXPERIMENTATION AND DEVELOPMENT- Taxable property or services used in an active trade or business for the purpose of research, experimentation and development shall be treated as purchased to produce taxable property or services.

`(3) INSURANCE PAYMENTS- Taxable property or services purchased by an insurance company on behalf of an insured shall be treated as a property or service purchased to produce a taxable property or service if the entire premium for the insurance contract giving rise to the insurer's obligation was subject to tax in accordance with subsection (a) (relating to financial intermediation services).

`(4) EDUCATION AND TRAINING- Education and training shall be treated as purchased to produce taxable property or services. For purposes of this section, education and training shall mean tuition for general primary, secondary, or university level education, and tuition for job-related training courses. Tuition shall not include amounts attributable to room or board for the student.

`(f) Qualified fixtures shall include only those fixtures that are a permanent, integral, incorporated and irremovable part of the structure and shall exclude furniture, furnishings, appliances or similar tangible personal property.

`(g) REAL PROPERTY- For purposes of this chapter, the term real property shall have the meaning ascribed to it at common law. The Secretary shall by regulation establish uniform national rules for purposes of administering this chapter to the extent that jurisdictions within the United States may provide different holdings as to the scope of the term real property.

`(h) RESIDENCE- Whenever this chapter requires that the State of `residence' need be determined, it shall be determined in descending order of priority as the State of permanent abode, the center of vital interests, or the habitual abode. If the State of residence is still undetermined, if the person is a resident of the United States, the determination will be made by the Federal Office of Revenue Allocation.

`(i) Residential real property is real property, including structures, land, and qualified fixtures and appurtenances thereto that--

　　`(1) is held in fee simple and

　　`(2) is predominantly used as a residence or dwelling.

`(j) SECRETARY- For purposes of this chapter, the term `Secretary' means the United States Secretary of Treasury.

`(k) STATE ADMINISTRATOR- For purposes of this chapter, the term `State Administrator' shall mean the highest State official responsible for administering the taxes imposed by this subtitle in the conforming State. In States that are not conforming States, the `State Administrator' shall mean the person designated by the Secretary as the Federal official responsible for administering the taxes imposed by this chapter in a non-conforming State. State Administrator shall also mean, when the context so requires, the Federal official responsible for administering the multi-State vendor program.

`(l) Structures, for purposes of subsection (i) shall include homes that are manufactured housing but not self-propelled and not on wheels.

`(m) TANGIBLE PERSONAL PROPERTY- For purposes of this chapter, the term tangible personal property shall have the meaning ascribed to it at common law. The Secretary shall by regulation establish uniform national rules for purposes of administering this chapter to the extent that jurisdictions within the United States may provide different holdings as to the scope of the term tangible personal property.

`(n) TAXABLE PROPERTY OR SERVICES-

　　`(1) GENERAL RULE- For purposes of this chapter, the term `taxable property or service' means--

`(A) any property (including leaseholds of any term or rents with respect to such property) other than intangible property, and

`(B) any service (including any financial intermediation services).

`(2) WAGES- For purposes of the preceding sentence, services shall not include wages paid by an employer engaged in an active trade or business that is registered pursuant to section 43. Services shall include wages paid by an employer (including government employers) not engaged in an active trade or business unless those wages are paid by a qualified not-for-profit organization (as defined in section 3(a)(2)(C).

`(3) INTANGIBLE PROPERTY-

`(A) IN GENERAL- For purposes of this subtitle, intangible property shall include copyrights, trademarks, patents, goodwill, financial instruments, and other property deemed intangible at common law.

`(B) CERTAIN TYPES OF PROPERTY- For purposes of this subtitle, intangible property shall not include tangible personal property (or rents or leaseholds of any term thereon), real property (or rents or leaseholds of any term thereon), and computer software.

`(C) ANTI-AVOIDANCE RULE- Notwithstanding subparagraph (A), the sale of a copyright or trademark shall be treated as the sale of taxable services (within the meaning of section 1) if the substance of the transaction selling said copyright or trademark constituted the sale of the services that produced the copyrighted material or the trademark.

`(o) UNITED STATES- For purposes of this chapter, the term `United States', when used in the geographical sense, means the 50 States, the District of Columbia, and any commonwealth, territory or possession of the United States.

`SEC. 22. SPECIAL RULES.

`(a) FOREIGN FINANCIAL INTERMEDIATION SERVICES-

`(1) SPECIAL RULES RELATING TO INTERNATIONAL FINANCIAL INTERMEDIATION SERVICES- Financial intermediation services shall be deemed as used or consumed within the United States if the person (or any related party within the meaning of section 2(e)) purchasing the services is a resident of the United States.

`(2) Any person that provides financial intermediation services to United States residents must, as a condition of lawfully providing such services, designate, in a form prescribed by the Secretary, a United States tax representative. This United States tax representative shall be responsible for ensuring that the taxes imposed by this chapter are collected and remitted an shall be jointly and severally liable for collecting and remitting these taxes. The Secretary may require reasonable bond of the United States tax representative.

`(b) FINANCING LEASES-

`(1) DEFINED- For purposes of this section, a financing lease shall be any lease under which the lessee shall have the right to acquire the property

for 50 percent or less of its fair market value at the end of the lease term.

`(2) TAX- Financing leases shall be taxed in the method set forth in this section.

`(3) DETERMINATION OF PRINCIPLE AND INTEREST COMPONENTS OF FINANCING LEASE- The Secretary shall promulgate rules for disaggregating the principle and interest components of a financing lease. The principle amount shall be determined to the extent possible by examination of the contemporaneous sales price or prices of the same or similar property as the leased property.

`(4) ALTERNATIVE METHOD- In the event that contemporaneous sales prices of the same or similar property as the lease property are not available, the principle and interest components of a financing lease shall be disaggregating using the applicable interest rate (as defined in section 28), plus 4 percent.

`(5) PRINCIPAL COMPONENT- The principal component of the financing lease shall be subject to tax as if a purchase in the amount of the principal component had been made on the day the lease was entered into.

`(6) INTEREST COMPONENT- The financial intermediation services amount with respect to the interest component of the financing lease shall be subject to tax.

`(7) COORDINATION- If the principal component and financial intermediation services amount with respect to the interest component of a lease have been taxed pursuant to this section, then the gross lease or rental payments shall not be subject to additional tax.

`(c) Installment Sales, Accounting, Returns-

`(1) GENERAL RULE- Tax will be due when payment for the taxable property and services sold, consumed, used or enjoyed is actually received.

`(2) ALTERNATIVE RULE- A vendor may elect to adopt the accrual method of accounting for purposes of determining when the tax will be due. Said election must apply to all sales made by vendor in a particular calendar year.

`(3) INSTALLMENT SALES- Tax will be due on taxable property and services sold under the installment method when payment for the taxable property and services sold is actually received.

`(4) RETURNS- A credit shall be provided to the vendor for returned taxable property and services when actual payment for the returned taxable property and services is made by the vendor to the person returning the taxable property and services.

`(d) MIXED USE PROPERTY OR SERVICES-

`(1) MIXED USE PROPERTY OR SERVICE DEFINED- Mixed Use Property or Service is taxable property or services purchased both for a purpose that would give rise to an exemption pursuant to section 2 and for taxable use, consumption or enjoyment.

`(2) EXEMPTION THRESHOLD- Mixed Use Property or Service shall not be exempt pursuant to section 2 unless said property is used more than 95 percent for purposes that would give rise to an exemption pursuant to section 2.

`(3) MIXED USE PROPERTY OR SERVICES CREDIT- A business registered pursuant to section 43 is entitled to a business use conversion credit (pursuant to section 11(d)) equal to product of--

`(A) the mixed use property amount,

`(B) the business use ratio, and

`(C) the rate of tax imposed by section 1.

`(4) MIXED USE PROPERTY AMOUNT- The mixed use property amount for each year shall be--

`(A) one-thirtieth of the purchase price for real property for thirty years or until the property is sold,

`(B) one-seventh of the purchase price for tangible personal property for seven years or until the property is sold,

`(C) one-fifth of the purchase price for vehicles for five years or until the property is sold, and

`(D) a reasonable amount for other types of taxable property or services or in accordance with regulations.

`(5) BUSINESS USE RATIO- The business use ratio is the ratio of business use to total use for a particular year. For vehicles, the business use ratio will be the ratio of business purpose miles to total miles. For real property, the business use ratio is the ratio of floor space used for business purposes to total floor space. For tangible personal property (except for vehicles), the business use ratio is the ratio of total time used for business purposes to total time used. For other property or services, the business ratio shall be calculated using a reasonable method. Reasonable records must be maintained to support a taxpayer's business use of the mixed use property or service.

`(e) GAMING- There is hereby imposed a 15-percent tax on taxable gaming services. Taxable gaming services shall be the gross gaming receipts less total gaming payoffs. This tax shall be paid and remitted by the person offering the gaming services.

`SEC. 23. DETERMINATION OF FINANCIAL INTERMEDIATION SERVICES AMOUNT.

`(a) FINANCIAL INTERMEDIATION SERVICES- For purposes of this subtitle--

`(1) IN GENERAL- The term `financial intermediation services' means the sum of--

`(A) explicitly charged financial intermediation services, and

`(B) implicitly charged financial intermediation services.

`(2) EXPLICITLY CHARGED FINANCIAL INTERMEDIATION SERVICES- The term `explicitly charged financial intermediation services' includes--

`(A) brokerage fees,

`(B) explicitly stated banking, loan origination, processing, documentation, credit check fees or other similar fees,

`(C) safe-deposit box fees,

`(D) insurance premiums, to the extent such premiums are not allocable to the investment account of the underlying insurance policy,

`(E) trustees' fees, and

`(F) other financial service fees (including, but not limited to, mutual fund management, sales, and exit fees).

`(3) IMPLICITLY CHARGED FINANCIAL INTERMEDIATION SERVICES-

`(A) IN GENERAL- The term `implicitly charged financial intermediation services' includes the gross imputed amount in relation to any underlying interest bearing investment, account, or debt.

`(B) GROSS IMPUTED AMOUNT- For purposes of subparagraph (A), the term `gross imputed amount' means--

`(i) with respect to any underlying interest bearing investment or account, the product of--

>`(I) the excess (if any) of the basic interest rate (as defined in section 27) over the rate paid on such investment, and

>`(II) such account balance, and

>`(ii) with respect to any underlying interest bearing debt, the product of--

>`(I) the excess (if any) of the rate paid on such debt over the basic interest rate (as defined in section 27), and

>`(II) such debt balance.

`(b) For purposes of section 1(c), the seller of financial intermediation services shall be--

>`(1) in the case of explicitly charged financial intermediation services (as defined in subsection (a)(2)), the person who receives the gross payments for the charged financial intermediation services,

>`(2) in the case of implicit financial intermediation services (as defined in subsection (a)(3)) with respect to any underlying interest bearing investment or account, the person making the interest payments on the interest bearing investment or account, and

>`(3) in the case of implicit financial intermediation services (as defined in subsection (a)(2)) with respect to any interest bearing debt, the person receiving the interest payments on the interest bearing debt.

`SEC. 24. BAD DEBTS.

`(a) For purposes of section 11, a bad debt shall be a business loan or debt that becomes wholly or partially worthless.

`(b) For purposes of subsection (a), a business loan or debt is a bona fide loan or debt made for a business purpose that both parties intended be repaid.

`(c) No loan or debt shall be considered wholly or partially worthless unless it has been in arrears for 90 days or more, provided, however, that if a debt is discharged wholly or partially in bankruptcy before 90 days has elapsed, then it shall be deemed wholly or partially worthless on the date of discharge.

`(d) A loan or debt that has been in arrears for 90 days or more may be deemed wholly or partially worthless by the holder unless a payment schedule has been entered into between the debtor and the lender.

`(e) CROSS REFERENCE-

>`For tax on subsequent payments, see section 11(g)(3).

`SEC. 25. TIMING OF TAX ON FINANCIAL INTERMEDIATION SERVICES.

`The tax on financial intermediation services provided in connection to an underlying investment account

or debt shall be calculated and collected with the same frequency that statements are rendered by the financial institution in connection with the investment account or debt but not less frequently than quarterly.

`SEC. 26. ALTERNATIVE METHOD FOR CALCULATING TAX DUE.

`(a) ALTERNATIVE METHOD PERMISSIBLE- A provider of financial intermediation services need not calculate its liability on a transaction-by-transaction or account-by-account basis provided that the method used by the financial intermediation services provider--

`(1) is reasonable, and

`(2) will lead to a tax liability that is substantially similar to that projected under ordinary sales tax principles. The provider of financial intermediation services shall set forth his proposed method and the reasons why it meets the criteria set forth in the preceding sentence in a petition to the Secretary.

`(b) SECRETARY TO RULE- An alternative method proposed in a petition pursuant to subsection (a) shall be accepted by the Secretary unless the Secretary rules that the proposed alternative method--

`(1) is unreasonable, or

`(2) will lead to a tax liability that is substantially different from that projected under ordinary sales tax principles.

The Secretary shall set froth the reasons for his ruling in a finding. The Secretary must make his ruling within 120 days of receiving the petition and notify the petitioner of his decision. In the event the Secretary fails to render a ruling within 120 days, then the proposed method shall be permissible. He must provide the petitioner with a copy of the finding within 30 days of a ruling. He must publish the permissible method (including those methods that become permissible by virtue of the Secretary's failure to rule).

`(c) EFFECTIVE DATES OF ALTERNATIVE METHOD- An alternative method ruled permissible or permissible by virtue of the Secretary's failure to rule shall be effective indefinitely and may take effect as early as the month after the alternative method becomes permissible. The Secretary may, however, after an investigation, audit, or otherwise, subsequently rule on his own initiative that the method is not permissible. Such subsequent ruling shall be prospective in effect and not take effect until the latter of--

`(1) the first day of the calendar year following the ruling, or

`(2) 120 days after the ruling.

If judicial review is sought pursuant to subsection (d), said subsequent ruling shall not take effect until a final judgment is rendered by the court.

`(d) JUDICIAL REVIEW- A ruling by the Secretary with respect to a petition for use of an alternative method pursuant to subsection (a) shall be subject to judicial review in any court of competent jurisdiction, provided, however, that the standard of review shall be whether the petitioner establishes by clear and convincing evidence that the decision of the Secretary should be reversed.

`(e) REGULATIONS- The Secretary may provide by regulation permissible alternative methods for calculating tax due including methods based on annual flows of revenue and expense.

`SEC. 27. BASIC INTEREST RATE.

`For purposes of this subchapter, the basic interest rate with respect to a debt instrument, investment, financing lease, or account shall be the applicable interest rate (as determined in section 28). For debt instruments, investments, or accounts of contractually fixed interest, the applicable interest rate of the month of issuance shall apply. For debt instruments, investments, or accounts of variable interest rates and which have no reference interest rate, the applicable interest rate shall be the Federal short-term interest rate for each month. For debt instruments, investments or accounts of variable interest rates and which have a reference interest rate, the applicable interest rate shall be the applicable interest rate for the reference interest rate for each month.

`SEC. 28. APPLICABLE INTEREST RATE.

`(a) IN GENERAL-

`(1) In the case of a debt instrument, investment, financing lease, or account with a term of not over 3 years, the applicable interest rate is the Federal short-term rate.

`(2) In the case of a debt instrument, investment, financing lease, or account with a term of over 3 years but not over 9 years, the applicable interest rate is the Federal mid-term rate.

`(3) In the case of a debt instrument, investment, financing lease, or account with a term of over 9 years, the applicable interest rate is the Federal long-term rate.

`(b) FEDERAL SHORT-TERM RATE- The Federal short-term rate shall be the rate determined by the Secretary based on the average market yield (during any 1 month) on outstanding marketable obligations of the United States with remaining periods to maturity of 3 years or less.

`(c) FEDERAL MID-TERM RATE- The Federal mid-term rate determined by the Secretary based on the average market yield (during any 1 month) on outstanding marketable obligations of the United States with remaining periods to maturity of more than 3 years and not over 9 years.

`(d) FEDERAL LONG-TERM RATE- The Federal long-term rate shall be the rate determined by the Secretary based on the average market yield (during any 1 month) on outstanding marketable obligations of the United States with remaining periods to maturity of over 9 years.

`(e) DETERMINATION OF RATES- During each calendar month, the Secretary shall determine the Federal short-term rate, the Federal mid-term rate, and the Federal long-term rate which shall apply during the following calendar month.

`Subchapter D--Authority for States to Collect Tax

`Sec. 31. Authority for States to collect tax.

`Sec. 32. Federal administrative support for States.

`Sec. 33. Federal administration option for multi-State vendors.

`Sec. 34. General administrative matters.

`SEC. 31. AUTHORITY FOR STATES TO COLLECT TAX.

`(a) IN GENERAL- The tax imposed by this chapter on gross payments for the use, consumption or enjoyment of taxable property or services within a State which is an administering State shall be administered, collected, and remitted to the United States Treasury by such State.

`(b) ADMINISTERING STATE- For purposes of this section, the term `administering State' means any State--

`(1) which maintains a conforming sales tax, and

`(2) which enters into a cooperative agreement with the Secretary containing reasonable provisions, limited in scope and detail, governing the administration by such State of the taxes imposed by this chapter and the remittance to the United States in a timely manner of taxes collected under this chapter.

`(c) CONFORMING SALES TAX- For purposes of subsection (b), a State maintains a conforming sales tax if such State imposes, administers, and collects a sales tax--

`(1) which conforms to the tax imposed by this chapter in all significant respects (other than the rate of tax), including--

`(A) the same taxable property and services,

`(B) the same exemptions, and

`(C) the same credits and refunds (other than section 11(a)(4) (relating to the taxpayer administrative credit) and section 13 (relating to the family consumption refund)), and

`(2) which is imposed at a rate of no less than 1 percent.

`(d) COOPERATIVE AGREEMENTS- The agreement under subsection (b)(2) shall be limited in scope and detail but include provisions for the expeditious transfer of funds, contact officers, dispute resolution, information exchange, confidentiality, taxpayer rights, and other matters of importance.

`(e) TIMELY REMITTANCE OF TAX-

`(1) IN GENERAL- Administering States shall remit and pay over taxes collected under this chapter on behalf of the United States (less the administration fee allowable under paragraph (2)) no later than 15 days after receipt.

`(2) ADMINISTRATION FEE- Administering States may retain an administration fee equal to one percent of the amounts otherwise required to be remitted to the United States under this chapter by the State.

`(f) LIMITATION ON ADMINISTRATION OF TAX BY UNITED STATES- The Secretary may administer the tax imposed by this chapter in an administering State only if--

`(1)(A) such State has failed on a regular and sustained basis to timely remit to the United States taxes collected under this chapter on behalf of the United States, or

`(B) such State has on a regular and sustained basis otherwise materially breached the agreement referred to in subsection (b)(2),

`(2) the State has failed to cure such failures and alleged breaches within a reasonable time,

`(3) the Secretary provides such State with written notice of such failures and alleged breaches, and

`(4) a district court of the United States within such State has rendered a decision permitting such administration.

`(g) The Secretary shall administer the tax imposed by this chapter in any State or other jurisdiction that is not an administering State.

`(h) It shall be permissible for a conforming State to contract with another conforming State to administer its sales tax for an agreed fee. In this case, the agreement contemplated by subsection (d) shall have both States and the Federal

Government as parties.

`(i) Coordination Among Conforming States-

`(1) EXEMPTION CERTIFICATES- Conforming States shall honor exemption certificates issued by other conforming States.

`(2) AUDITS- Conforming States shall not conduct audits at facilities in other Conforming States but shall instead cooperate with other Conforming States using the mechanisms established by section 32 of this subchapter or by other agreement or Compact.

`SEC. 32. FEDERAL ADMINISTRATIVE SUPPORT FOR STATES.

`(a) The Secretary shall administer a program to facilitate information sharing among States.

`(b) The Secretary shall facilitate and may be a party to a Compact Among Conforming States for purposes of facilitating the taxation of interstate purchases and for other purposes that may facilitate implementation of this chapter.

`(c) The Secretary shall have the authority to promulgate regulations and guidelines to assist States in administering the national sales tax, to provide for uniformity in the administration of the tax and to provide guidance to taxpayers and administrators.

`SEC. 33. FEDERAL ADMINISTRATION OPTION FOR MULTISTATE VENDORS.

`(a) IN GENERAL- Vendors that maintain retail establishments in five or more conforming States may elect, in a form prescribed by the Secretary, to have their sales tax obligations administered by the Federal Government under the multistate vendor program.

`(b) FEDERAL GOVERNMENT TO COLLECT AND REMIT STATE SALES TAXES- Under the multistate vendor program, the Federal Government will collect Federal and conforming State sales taxes and remit the State sales taxes to the States within 10 days of receiving said revenue.

`(c) FEDERAL ADMINISTRATION- The Federal Government will serve in the place of the State Administrator with respect to multi-State vendors exercising the election under this section. With respect to electing multi-State vendors, the Federal Government exclusively will--

`(1) audit;

`(2) provide certificates; and

`(3) otherwise administer the Federal and conforming State sales tax in place of the administering State.

`SEC. 34. GENERAL ADMINISTRATIVE MATTERS.

`(a) IN GENERAL- The Secretary and each State Administrator may employ accountants, auditors, investigators, assistants, and clerks for the administration of this subtitle and may delegate to employees the authority to conduct interviews, hearings, prescribe rules, promulgate regulations, and perform such other duties as are required by this subtitle.

`(b) RESOLUTION OF ANY INCONSISTENT RULES AND REGULATIONS- In the event that the Secretary and any State Administrator have issued inconsistent rules or regulations, the rule or regulation issued by the Secretary shall govern provided that the Secretary possessed the statutory authority to issue the rule or regulation.

`(c) ADEQUATE NOTICE TO BE PROVIDED- Except in the case of an emergency declared by the Secretary (and not his designee), no rule or regulation issued by the Secretary with respect to any internal revenue law shall take effect before 90 days have elapsed after its publication in the Federal Register. Upon issuance, the Secretary shall provide copies of all rules or regulations issued under this title to each sales tax administering authority.

`(d) NO RULES, RULINGS, OR REGULATIONS WITH RETROACTIVE EFFECT-

> `(1) IN GENERAL- No rule, ruling, or regulation issued or promulgated by the Secretary relating to any internal revenue law or by a State Administrator that constitutes a change in law (including a reversal of prior law and new law) shall be retroactive in effect.

> `(2) Notwithstanding paragraph (1), a rule, ruling, or regulation that provides guidance or clarifies existing law may lawfully apply to cases prior to its issuance.

> `(3) For purposes of this subsection, the term `law' includes State and Federal statutes, regulations, rules, rulings, and court decisions.

> `(4) A rule, ruling, or regulation issued in contravention to paragraph (1) shall be void as to taxable events arising prior to the issuance of such rule, ruling, or regulation.

> `(5) REVIEW OF IMPACT OF RULES, RULINGS, AND REGULATIONS ON SMALL BUSINESS-

>> `(A) SUBMISSION TO SMALL BUSINESS ADMINISTRATION- After publication of any proposed or temporary regulation by the Secretary relating to internal revenue laws, the Secretary shall submit such regulation to the Chief Counsel for Advocacy of the Small Business Administration for comment on the impact of such regulation on small businesses. Not later than the date 4 weeks after the date of such submission, the Chief Counsel for Advocacy of the

Small Business Administration shall submit comments on such regulation to the Secretary.

> `(B) CONSIDERATION OF COMMENTS- In prescribing any final regulation which supersedes a proposed or temporary regulation which had been submitted under this subsection to the Chief Counsel for Advocacy of the Small Business Administration, the Secretary shall--
>
> > `(i) consider the comments of the Chief Counsel for Advocacy of the Small Business Administration on such proposed or temporary regulation, and
> >
> > `(ii) discuss any response to such comments in the preamble to the regulation.
>
> `(C) SUBMISSION OF CERTAIN FINAL REGULATIONS- In the case of promulgation by the Secretary of any final regulations (other than a temporary regulation) which do not supersede a proposed regulation, the requirements of subparagraphs (A) and (B) shall apply, except that the submission under subparagraph (A) shall be made at least 4 weeks before the date of such promulgation, and the consideration and discussion required under subparagraph (B) shall be made in connection with the promulgation of such final regulation.

`Subchapter E--Other Administrative Provisions

`Sec. 41. Monthly reports and payments.

`Sec. 42. Records.

`Sec. 43. Registration.

`Sec. 44. Certificates.

`Sec. 45. Penalties.

`Sec. 46. Burden of persuasion and burden of production.

`Sec. 47. Attorneys and accountancy fees.

`Sec. 48. Appeals.

`Sec. 49. Taxpayer subject to subpoena on production.

`Sec. 50. Tax Court jurisdiction.

`Sec. 51. Power to levy.

`Sec. 52. Problem resolution officers.

`SEC. 41. MONTHLY REPORTS AND PAYMENTS.

`(a) REPORTS- On or before the 20th of each month, every person who is liable to collect and remit the tax imposed by this chapter, or pay the tax imposed by this chapter by reason of gross payments described in section (1) (hereafter in this section referred to as the `taxpayer'), shall submit to the appropriate tax authority (in a form satisfactory to the Secretary) a report relating to the previous month that sets forth--

`(1) the gross payments referred to in section 1,

`(2) the tax collected under this chapter in connection with such payments, and

`(3) the amount and type of any credit claimed.

`(b) PAYMENTS OF TAX- The tax imposed by this chapter with respect to any use, consumption or enjoyment during any month shall be paid on or before the 20th of the succeeding month. One payment shall pay both Federal and conforming State tax liability.

`(c) INTEREST ON AMOUNTS REMITTED LATE-

`(1) IN GENERAL- If any amount required to be paid on or before the 20th of any month is paid after such 20th day, the taxpayer shall pay simple interest from such 20th day at the rate of--

`(A) 1 percent per month (or any fraction thereof) for the first month, and

`(B) 1.5 percent per month (or any fraction thereof) thereafter.

`(2) AMOUNTS PAID AFTER COLLECTION ACTION-

`(A) IN GENERAL- The rate of interest under paragraph (1) shall be 2 percent per month (or any fraction thereof) with respect to amounts paid only after the commencement of a collection action with respect to such amounts.

`(B) COLLECTION ACTION- For purposes of subparagraph (A), the term `collection action' includes administrative levies or garnishments

and the commencement of legal action in any court.

`(d) PENALTY FOR LATE FILING-

`(1) IN GENERAL- In the case of a failure by any person to file a report required by subsection (a) on or before due date (determined with regard to any extension) for such report, such person shall pay a penalty equal to the greater of--

`(A) $50, or

`(B) 0.5 percent of the gross payments referred to in section 1 required to be shown on the report.

`(2) INCREASED PENALTY ON RETURNS FILED AFTER WRITTEN INQUIRY- The amount of the penalty under paragraph (1) shall be doubled with respect to any report filed after a written inquiry with respect to such report is received by the taxpayer from the State Administrator.

`(3) Exceptions-

`(A) REASONABLE CAUSE- No penalty shall be imposed under paragraph (1) with respect to any failure if it is shown that such failure is due to reasonable cause.

`(B) OTHER WAIVER AUTHORITY- In addition to penalties not imposed by reason of subparagraph (A), the State Administrator, on application, shall waive the penalty imposed by paragraph (1) once per taxpayer per 2-year period. The preceding sentence shall not apply to a penalty determined under paragraph (2).

`(e) EXTENSIONS FOR FILING REPORTS-

`(1) AUTOMATIC EXTENSIONS FOR LESS THAN 30 DAYS- On application, extensions of less than 30 days to file reports under subsection (a) shall be automatically granted.

`(2) OTHER EXTENSIONS- Extensions of 30 to 90 days to file such reports shall be liberally granted by the State Administrator for reasonable cause. Extensions greater than 90 days may be granted by the State Administrator to avoid hardship.

`(3) NO EXTENSION FOR PAYMENT OF TAXES- Notwithstanding paragraphs (1) and (2), no extension shall be granted with respect to the time for paying the taxes under this chapter.

`(f) PENALTY FOR WILLFULLY OR RECKLESSLY ACCEPTING A FALSE EXEMPTION CERTIFICATE- A person who willingly or recklessly accepts a false exemption certificate shall pay a penalty equal to 20 percent of the tax not collected on gross payments for taxable property and services by virtue of said acceptance.

`(g) The Secretary shall establish a system whereby violation of the National Retail Sales Tax Act of 1997 can be brought to the attention of the Secretary for investigation through the use of a toll-free telephone number and otherwise.

`SEC. 42. RECORDS.

`Any person liable to collect and remit taxes pursuant to this chapter or pay the tax imposed by this chapter by reason of gross payments described in section 1, shall keep records (including, but not limited to, copies of all section 54 receipts provided and complete records of exempt purchases including exempt purchaser's exemption certificates and tax number and the net of tax amount of purchase) sufficient to provide a reasonable basis for determining the amounts reported, collected, and remitted for a period of 3 years after the filing of the report for which the records formed the basis. Any purchaser who purchased taxable property or services but did not pay tax by reason of asserting an exemption shall keep records sufficient to provide a reasonable basis for determining whether the exemption was valid for a period of 3 years after the purchase of taxable property or services.

`SEC. 43. REGISTRATION.

`(a) IN GENERAL- Any person liable to collect and remit taxes pursuant to section 1 who is engaged in an active trade or business shall register with the State or Federal taxing authorities administering the taxes imposed by this chapter.

`(b) DESIGNATION OF TAX MATTERS PERSON- Every person registered pursuant to subsection (a) shall designate a tax matters person. Each person registered must provide notice of a change in the identity of the tax matters person within 30 days of said change.

`SEC. 44. CERTIFICATE.

`The State Administrator shall issue certificates of registration and qualification certificates to qualified not-for-profit organizations and may issue such other certificates as may prove useful in the administration of the taxes imposed by this chapter.

`SEC. 45. PENALTIES.

`(a) FAILURE TO REGISTER- Each person who is required to register pursuant to section 43 but fails to do so prior to notification by the State Administrator shall be liable for a penalty of $500.

`(b) Failure To Collect or Remit Tax-

`(1) CIVIL PENALTY- Each person who recklessly or willfully fails to collect or remit taxes imposed by section 1 shall be liable for a penalty equal to the greater of $500 or 20 percent of the tax not collected or remitted.

`(2) CRIMINAL PENALTY- Each person who willfully fails as part of an active trade or business to collect or remit taxes imposed by this chapter may be imprisoned for a period of up to one year.

`(c) FAILURE TO PAY TAX-

`(1) CIVIL PENALTY- Each person who willfully fails to pay taxes imposed by section 1 shall be liable for a penalty equal to the greater of $500 or 20 percent of the tax not paid.

`(2) CRIMINAL PENALTY- Each person who willfully fails to pay taxes imposed by this chapter may be imprisoned for a period of up to six months.

`SEC. 46. BURDEN OF PERSUASION AND BURDEN OF PRODUCTION.

`In all disputes concerning taxes imposed by this chapter, the person engaged in a dispute with the State Administrator shall have the burden of production of documents and records but the State Administrator shall have the burden of persuasion. In all disputes concerning the legitimacy of an exemption claimed by a purchaser, if the seller has on file a copy of a bona fide exemption certificate and did not have reasonable cause to believe that an exemption from the tax was unavailable to the

purchaser with respect to such purchase, then the burden of production of documents and records relating to that exemption shall rest with the purchaser and not with the seller.

`SEC. 47. ATTORNEYS AND ACCOUNTANCY FEES.

`In all disputes concerning taxes imposed by this chapter, the person engaged in a dispute with the State Administrator or the Secretary, as the case may be, shall be entitled to reasonable attorneys and accountancy fees incurred in direct relation to the dispute unless the State Administrator or the Secretary, as the case may be, establishes that his position was substantially justified.

`SEC. 48. APPEALS.

`The State Administrator and the Secretary shall establish an administrative appeals process wherein the taxpayer is provided a full and fair hearing in connection with any disputes he has with the State Administrator or the Secretary.

`SEC. 49. TAXPAYER SUBJECT TO SUBPOENA ON PRODUCTION.

`Taxpayers are subject to subpoena for records and documents required by the State Administrator or the Secretary, as the case may be, to accurately determine liability for tax under this chapter.

`SEC. 50. TAX COURT JURISDICTION.

`The United States Tax Court shall have jurisdiction pursuant to section 7442 in connection with all disputes with taxpayers arising under this chapter.

`SEC. 51. POWER TO LEVY.

`Pursuant to enforcement of a judgment duly rendered by a court of law, the State Administrator or the Secretary, as the case may be, shall have the right to levy and seize property and garnish wages to collect amounts due under this chapter.

`SEC. 52. PROBLEM RESOLUTION OFFICERS.

`The State Administrator shall establish a Problem Resolution Office. Problem Resolution Officers shall have the authority to investigate taxpayer complaints and enjoin collection activity if, in the opinion of the Problem Resolution Officer, said collection activity is reasonably likely to not be in compliance with law. Said administrative injunction may only be reversed by the highest official in the relevant State or Federal taxing authority or by its General Counsel upon a finding that the collection activity is justified by clear and convincing evidence. The authority to reverse this administrative injunction may not be delegated. Problem Resolution Officers shall not be disciplined or adversely affected for the issuance of administrative injunctions unless a pattern or issuing injunctions that are manifestly unreasonable is proven in an administrative hearing. Nothing in this section shall limit the authority of the State Administrators or the taxpayer to pursue any legal remedy in any court with jurisdiction over the dispute at issue.

`SEC. 53. JURISDICTION AND INTERSTATE ALLOCATION.

`(a) ALLOCATION RULES- For purposes of allocating revenue between or among administering states from taxes imposed by this subtitle, the revenue shall be allocated to those states that are the destination of the taxable property or services. The destination of the purchase of taxable property and services shall be determined in accordance with this section.

`(b) FEDERAL OFFICE OF REVENUE ALLOCATION- The Secretary shall establish an Office of Revenue Allocation to arbitrate any claims or disputes among administering states as to the destination of taxable property and services for purposes of allocating revenue between or among the states from taxes imposed by this subtitle. The determination of the Administrator of the Office of Revenue Allocation shall be subject to judicial review in any federal court with competent jurisdiction provided, however, that the standard of review shall be abuse of discretion.

`(c) TANGIBLE PERSONAL PROPERTY- The destination of tangible personal property shall be the state or territory in which the property was first delivered to the purchaser. Tangible personal property shipped by means of the mail or common carrier shall be deemed delivered to the location of the purchaser for purposes of this subsection upon shipment by mail or common carrier.

`(d) REAL PROPERTY- The destination of real property or rents or leaseholds on real property shall be state or territory in which the real property is located.

`(e) OTHER PROPERTY- The destination of other property shall be residence of the purchaser.

`(f) Services-

> `(1) GENERAL RULE- The destination of services shall be state or territory in which the use, consumption or enjoyment of the services occurred. Allocation of service invoices relating to more than one jurisdiction shall be on the basis of time.

> `(2) TELECOMMUNICATIONS SERVICES- The destination of telecommunications services shall be the residence of the purchaser. Telecommunications services shall include telephone, telegraph, cable television, satellite and computer on-line or network services.

> `(3) DOMESTIC TRANSPORTATION SERVICES- For transportation services where all of the final destinations are within the United States, the

destination of transportation services shall be the final destination of the trip (in the case of round or multiple trip fares, the services amount shall be equally allocated among the final destinations).

> `(4) INTERNATIONAL TRANSPORTATION SERVICES- For transportation services where the final destination or origin of the trip is without the United States, the service amount shall be deemed 50 percent attributable to the United States destination or origin.

`(g) FINANCIAL INTERMEDIATION SERVICES- The destination of financial intermediation services shall be the residence of the purchase.

`(h) A State Tax Administrator shall have jurisdiction over any gross payments made which have a destination (as determined in accordance with this section) within the state of said State Tax Administrator. This grant of jurisdiction is not exclusive of other jurisdiction that said State Tax Administrator may have.

`(i) RENTS AND ROYALTIES PAID FOR THE LEASE OF TANGIBLE PROPERTY-

> `(1) GENERAL RULE- The destination of rents and royalties paid for the lease of tangible property shall be where the property is located.

> `(2) VEHICLES- The destination of rent and lease payments on vehicles shall be--

>> `(A) in the case of rentals and leases of a term one month or less, the location where the vehicle was originally delivered to the lessee; and

>> `(B) in the case of rentals and leases of a term greater than one month, the residence of the lessee.

`SEC. 54. TAX TO BE STATED AND CHARGED SEPARATELY.

`(a) IN GENERAL- For each purchase of taxable property or services for which a tax is imposed pursuant to section 1, the sales tax shall be charged separately from the purchase price by the vendor or seller. For purchase of taxable property or services for which a tax is imposed pursuant to section 1, the vendor shall provide to the purchaser a receipt that sets forth at least the following information:

`(1) The property or services price exclusive of tax.

`(2) The amount of tax paid.

`(3) The property or service price inclusive of tax.

`(4) The tax rate (the amount of tax paid (per subparagraph 2) divided by the property or service price inclusive of tax (per subparagraph 3)).

`(5) The date that the good or service was sold.

`(6) The name of the vendor.

`(7) The vendor registration number.

`(b) VENDING MACHINE EXCEPTION- The requirements of subsection (a) shall be inapplicable in the case of sales by vending machines. Vending machines for purposes of this subsection shall mean machines--

`(1) that dispense taxable property in exchange for coins, one, five, ten or twenty dollar bills, and

`(2) that sell no single item exceeding ten dollars per unit in price.

`SEC. 55. INSTALLMENT AGREEMENTS; COMPROMISES.

`The State Administrator or the Secretary, as the case may be, is authorized to enter into written agreements with any person under which the person is allowed to satisfy liability for payment of any tax in installment payments if he determines that such agreement will facilitate the collection of such liability. The agreement shall remain in effect for the term of the agreement unless the information that the person provided to the Secretary or the State Administrator was materially inaccurate or incomplete. The Secretary and the State Administrator may compromise any amounts alleged to be due.

`SEC. 56. ACCOUNTING.

`(a) CASH METHOD TO BE USED GENERALLY- Vendors and other persons shall remit taxes and report transactions with respect to the month for which payment was received or the tax imposed by this chapter otherwise becomes due.

`(b) ELECTION TO USE ACCRUAL METHOD- A person may elect with respect to a calendar year, in a form prescribed by the Secretary, to remit taxes and report transactions with respect to the month where a sale was invoiced and accrued.

`(c) Cross Reference-

`For rules relating to bad debts for vendors electing the accrual method, see section 11(g).

`SEC. 57. HOBBY ACTIVITIES.

`(a) The exemption afforded by section 2(a)(1) shall not be available for any taxable property or service used by a trade or business if that trade or business is not engaged in for profit.

`(b) If the trade or business has received gross payments for the sale of taxable property or services that exceed the sum of--

`(1) taxable property and services purchased,

`(2) wages paid, and

`(3) taxes paid,

in 2 or more of the most recent 4 calendar years during which it operated, then the business activity shall be conclusively deemed to be engaged in for profit.'.

SEC. 5. PHASE-OUT OF THE INTERNAL REVENUE SERVICE.

(a) Appropriations for any expenses of the Internal Revenue Service including processing income tax returns for years prior to the repeal of the income tax, revenue accounting, management, transfer of payroll tax data to the Social Security Administration and otherwise for years after fiscal year 2001 are not authorized.

(b) Section 7801 is amended by adding the following new subsections:

`(d) EXCISE TAX BUREAU- There shall be in the Department of Treasury an Excise Tax Bureau to administer those excise taxes not repealed by this Act.

`(e) SALES TAX BUREAU- There shall be in the Department of Treasury a Sales Tax Bureau to administer the national sales tax in those States where it is required pursuant to section 31(g), and to discharge other Federal duties and powers relating to the national sales tax (including those required by sections 32, 33, and 53(b)). The Office of Revenue Allocation shall be within the Sales Tax Bureau.'.

(c) Section 7801(b)(2) is amended to read as follows:

`(2) ASSISTANT GENERAL COUNSELS- The Secretary of the Treasury may appoint, without regard to the provisions of the civil service laws, and fix the duties of not more than 5 Assistant General Counsel.'.

(d) SHORT YEAR-

(1) For purposes of the Federal income tax, the tax imposed by section 1 and section 11 for taxable years ending June 30, 1999, shall be modified as set

forth in this subsection.

(2) For calendar year taxpayers, the dollar figures in section 1 and section 11 shall be reduced by dividing by 2 all dollar figures that would be applicable but for this subsection.

(3) For fiscal year taxpayers, the dollar figures in section 1 and section 11 shall be equal to the product of--

(A) the dollar amount that would be applicable but for this subsection, and

(B) the ratio that has as its numerator the number of months in the taxpayer's taxable year ending June 30, 1999, and as its denominator 12.

(4) The Secretary shall publish tax rate schedules in accordance with this subsection.

SEC. 6. SOCIAL SECURITY ADMINISTRATION TO COLLECT PAYROLL TAXES.

(a) Commencing January 1, 1999, the Social Security Administration shall collect and administer the taxes imposed pursuant to chapter 2 of subtitle A (relating to self employment income taxes) and subtitle C (relating to employment taxes) of the Internal Revenue Code of 1986.

(b) CROSS REFERENCES-

For revised rules relating to the self-employment tax, see section 7 of this Act.

For rules relating to revised withholding tax schedules and family consumption refund, see section 13.

SEC. 7. SELF-EMPLOYMENT TAX.

(a) Subsection 1402(a) of the Internal Revenue Code of 1986 is amended to read as follows:

`(a) IN GENERAL- `Self employment income' shall mean gross payments received in a calendar year from the sale of taxable property or services (without regard to exemption) less the sum in a calendar year of--

`(1) purchases of taxable property or services (without regard to exemption) in furtherance of a business purpose,

`(2) any wages paid (whether to the self-employed person or others) in furtherance of a business purpose,

`(3) unused transition amounts, and

`(4) undeducted negative self employment income amounts from prior periods.

`(b) TRANSITION AMOUNTS-

`(1) GENERAL RULE- The transition amount for the ten calendar years commencing in 1999 shall be the unrecovered basis amount as of the end of December 31, 1998 divided by ten.

`(2) UNRECOVERED BASIS AMOUNT- The unrecovered basis amount shall be remaining income tax basis relating to--

`(A) prior law section 167 property placed in service prior to January 1, 1999, and

`(B) inventory held as of the end of 1998 (including any amounts capitalized in accordance with prior law section 263A).'.

(b) CONFORMING AMENDMENTS- Subsections 1402(b) and 1402(c) are hereby repealed. Subsections 1402(d) et seq. are hereby renumbered as subsections 1402(b) et seq.

SEC. 8. SOCIAL SECURITY BENEFITS INDEXED ON SALES TAX INCLUSIVE BASIS.

Subparagraph (D) of paragraph (1) of subsection (i) of section 215 of the Social Security Act (42 U.S.C. 415) (relating to cost-of-living increases in Social Security benefits) is amended to read as follows:

`(D)(i) the term `CPI increase percentage', with respect to a base quarter or cost-of-living quarter in any calendar year, means the percentage (rounded to the nearest one-tenth of 1 percent) by which the Consumer Price Index for that quarter (as prepared by the Department of Labor) exceeds such index for the most recent prior calendar quarter which was a base quarter under subparagraph (A)(ii) or, if later, the most recent cost-of-living computation quarter under subparagraph (B);

`(ii) if the Consumer Price Index (as prepared by the Department of Labor) does not include the national sales tax paid, then the term `CPI increase percentage' with respect to a base quarter or cost-of-living quarter in any calendar year, means the percentage (rounded to the nearest one-tenth of 1 percent) by which the product of--

`(I) the Consumer Price Index for that quarter (as prepared by the Department of Labor); and

`(II) the national sales tax factor,

exceeds such index for the most recent prior calendar quarter which was a base quarter under subparagraph (A)(ii) or, if later, the most recent cost-of-living computation quarter under subparagraph (B); and

`(iii) for purposes of clause (ii), the `national sales tax factor' is equal to one plus the quotient that is--

`(I) the sales tax rate (as defined in section 1 of title 26), divided by

`(II) the quantity that is one minus the sales tax rate.'.

SEC. 9. COMPENSATING PAYMENTS TO CERTAIN PERSONS ON FIXED INCOME.

(a) COMPENSATING PAYMENT- Eligible persons (as defined in subsection (c)) shall receive a compensating payment (as defined in subsection (b)) provided that they comply with subsection (g) (relating to applications).

(b) COMPENSATING PAYMENT DEFINED- The term `compensating payment' means the product of the qualified fixed income payment amount (as defined in subsection (e)) and the excess inflation rate (as defined in subsection (f)).

(c) ELIGIBLE PERSON DEFINED- An eligible person is any person with respect to any calendar year who is entitled to--

(1) Social Security benefits; and

(2) qualified fixed income payments (as defined in subsection (d)).

(d) QUALIFIED FIXED INCOME PAYMENT DEFINED- A qualified fixed income payment is a payment received by--

(1) a beneficiary under a defined benefit plan (within the meaning of section 414(j) of the Internal Revenue Code as in effect prior to the enactment of this Act) whether sponsored by a private or Government employer; or

(2) by an annuitant pursuant to an annuity contract between the annuitant and a bona fide insurance company.

A payment pursuant to a plan or annuity contract is not a qualified fixed income payment if the payment varies with investment performance, interest rates, or inflation. Payments pursuant to an annuity contract entered into after June 30, 1999, shall not be qualified fixed income payments. Payments pursuant to a defined benefit plan to a beneficiary that had been a participant in said defined benefit plan (within the meaning of section 410 of the Internal Revenue Code as in effect prior to the enactment of this Act) for less than 5 years shall not be qualified fixed income payments.

(e) QUALIFIED FIXED INCOME PAYMENT AMOUNT- The qualified fixed income payment amount is 1/12 of qualified fixed income payments that an eligible person is entitled to receive during the calendar year subsequent to the year for which the compensating payment is calculated, provided, however, that the qualified fixed income payment amount shall not exceed $5,000.

(f) EXCESS INFLATION RATE DEFINED- The term `excess inflation rate' shall mean the excess, if any, of the consumer price index (all urban) during the 18-month period ending December 31, 2000, over the increase projected for the consumer price index (all urban) in the Office of Management and Budget baseline reported in the Budget of the United States for Fiscal Year 1999 for said 18-month period. The baseline assumption for the 6 months in 1999 shall be 1/2 of the assumed increase for the entire calendar year 1999.

(g) APPLICATION REQUIRED- In order to receive compensating payments, each eligible person must apply in a form prescribed by the Secretary of Health and Human Services and provide such documentation as the Secretary may reasonably require.

(h) MEANS OF PAYMENT- Each person entitled to a compensating payment shall receive the compensating payment with their Social Security benefit payment. The compensating payment shall be separately indicated but may be included in one check. The funds to make compensating payments shall come from the general fund.

(i) The Secretary of Health and Human Services may require insurers that are parties to annuity contracts and defined benefit plan sponsors to issue a statement to annuitants or plan participants including such information as the Secretary may require to determine the qualified fixed income payment amount.

SEC. 10. INTEREST.

Section 6621 of the Internal Revenue Code of 1986 is amended by striking the last sentence in section 6621(a)(1) and by striking `3' in section 6621(a)(2)(B) and substituting in its stead `2'.

SEC. 11. SUPERMAJORITY REQUIRED TO RAISE RATE.

(a) IN GENERAL- It shall not be in order in the House of Representatives or the Senate to consider any bill, joint resolution, amendment thereto, or conference report thereon that includes any provision that--

(1) increases any federal sales tax rate, and

(2) provides any exemption, deduction, credit or other benefit which results in a reduction in federal revenues.

(b) WAIVER OR SUSPENSION- This section may be waived or suspended in the House of Representatives or the Senate only by the affirmative vote of two-thirds of the Members, duly chosen and sworn.

END

APPENDIX E

Tax Code Termination Act

105th CONGRESS

2d Session

H. R. 3097

AN ACT

To terminate the Internal Revenue Code of 1986.

HR 3097 EH

105th CONGRESS

2d Session

H. R. 3097

AN ACT

To terminate the Internal Revenue Code of 1986.

Be it enacted by the Senate and House of Representatives of the United States of America in Congress assembled,

SECTION 1. SHORT TITLE.

This Act may be cited as the `Tax Code Termination Act'.

SEC. 2. TERMINATION OF INTERNAL REVENUE CODE OF 1986.

(a) IN GENERAL- No tax shall be imposed by the Internal Revenue Code of 1986--

(1) for any taxable year beginning after December 31, 2002; and

(2) in the case of any tax not imposed on the basis of a taxable year, on any taxable event or for any period after December 31, 2002.

(b) EXCEPTION- Subsection (a) shall not apply to taxes imposed by--

(1) chapter 2 of such Code (relating to tax on self-employment income);

(2) chapter 21 of such Code (relating to Federal Insurance Contributions Act); and

(3) chapter 22 of such Code (relating to Railroad Retirement Tax Act).

SEC. 3. NEW FEDERAL TAX SYSTEM.

(a) STRUCTURE- The Congress hereby declares that any new Federal tax system should be a simple and fair system that--

(1) applies a low rate to all Americans;

(2) provides tax relief for working Americans;

(3) protects the rights of taxpayers and reduces tax collection abuses;

(4) eliminates the bias against savings and investment;

(5) promotes economic growth and job creation; and

(6) does not penalize marriage or families.

(b) TIMING OF IMPLEMENTATION- In order to ensure an easy transition and effective implementation, the Congress hereby declares that any new Federal tax system should be approved by Congress in its final form no later than July 4, 2002.

Passed the House of Representatives June 17, 1998.

Attest:

Clerk.

END

Claitor's Law Books and Publishing Division, Inc.
3165 S. Acadian @ I-10, P.O. Box 261333
Baton Rouge, LA 70826-1333
Phone TOLL-FREE 1-800-274-1403
LA Customers 504-344-0476
Fax 504-344-0480

___ **YES! Please send me** ____ **additional copy(ies) of Tauzin's** *A National Retail Sales Tax* **@$10.00* ea.**

GPO Best Sellers by Claitor's Publishing

ALSO send:

_____ **#1. Occupational Outlook Handbook 1998-99 pa. $42.00*, hb $46.00***
_____ **#2. North Amer. Indus. Classif. System Manual 1997 pa. $36.00*, hb $38.00***
_____ **#3. Statistical Abstract of U.S. 1997 pa. $43.00*, hb.$51.00***
_____ **#4. US Govt. Manual 1997-98pa. $40.00***
_____ **#5. World Factbook 1997, pa. $59.00***
_____ #6. Social Security Handbook 1997, pa. $36.00*
_____ #7. High School Counselor's Handbook 1998-99, pa. $9.50*
_____ #8. Congressional Directory 1997-98, pa. $30.00*, hb. $43.00*
_____ #9. Dictionary of Occupational Titles 4th ed., 2 vols. pa. $50.00*, hb. $55.00*
_____ #10.DOT supp:Selected Characteristics of Occupations 1993, pa. $40.00*
_____ #11.OOH supp:Career Guide to Industries 1998-99, pa. $17.00*
_____ #12.OOH supp:Occupational Projections 1998, pa. $6.50*
_____ #13.Economic Report of the President 1998, pa. $20.00*
_____ #14.Criminal Justice Statistics 1996, pa. $56.00*
_____ #15.Taxpayer Relief Act of 1997, pa. $37.00*
_____ #16.Infant Care 1993, pa. $4.00*   *GPO's all-time-ever best-seller!*
_____ #17.Catalog of Fed. Dom. Assistance 1997, looseleaf $69.00
_____ #18.Code of Fed. Regs. (CFR). All vols. on hand--which do you want?
_____ #19.N.Amer.Indus.Class.Sys.1997 Govt.ed.,pa$28.50, hb. $32.50, GPO cd-rom $45.00
_____ #20.Statistical Abstract Supp:State/Metro Area Data Book 1998 $24.00
_____ #21.GPO Style Manual 1998 reprint, paper $24.00
_____ #22.Handling Traumatic Events,paper $4.00

Check us out on the World Wide Web at: **http://www.claitors.com**
Any questions? Drop us a line or place your order via email at: **claitors@claitors.com**

ORDER FORM

Date_____

CLAITOR'S LAW BOOKS & PUBLISHING DIV.
3165 S. Acadian at I-10, P.O. Box 261333
Baton Rouge, LA 70826-1333

*Please specify quantity in boxes above when ordering.

Company_____

Attention_____Phone_____

Address_____

City_____State_____Zip_____ __

Name (Printed)_____ Signature_____

*Add city and/or state tax if appropriate.

❑ Check enclosed. *Add $5.00 for 1ˢᵗ vol. delivery & insurance and $2.00 for each additional book, plus LA residents add city and/or state tax as appropriate.

❑ Charge/Open my account. (delete one)
    Acct # (if known)_____

❑ Charge my Visa or MCard(delete one) Exp Date_____
    Acct. #_____
    *Please show name to left exactly as on card.

❑ Phone TOLL-FREE 800-274-1403 outside LA
    LA Customers call 504-344-0476

❑ FAX ---- save time and postage. 504-344-0480

❑ e-mail: claitors@claitors.com YES! You may place
             your order by e-mail.

❑ Check out our web site at: http://www.claitors.com